To Carol and Joe,
friends and
co-pilgrims on
the path.
Love,
Dick

Journeys On Your Spiritual Path

By
Louis Richard Batzler

Hidden Valley Press
7051 Poole Jones Road
Frederick, Maryland 2170

Journeys On Your Spiritual Path

Please direct all inquiries to:
Hidden Valley Press
7051 Poole Jones Road
Frederick, Maryland 21701

Cover by Michael Halminski.
Sketches by the author.

First Printing, 1982

Printed by Hagerstown Bookbinding and Printing Co., Inc.

Printed in U.S.A.

Library of Congress Catalog Number: 82–082069

ISBN: 0-935710-04-3

Dedication

To Mother and Father
who
started me on my life's journey
and walked with me on the mountains
and in the valleys

Contents

Preface

I believe the primary purpose of human life is to know, love and serve God.

This book has been written to help persons realize this purpose in their own lives. If just one person is helped in realizing this purpose, then my effort and intention will be fulfilled.

This work has come to fruition through the love and encouragement of many friends who have journeyed with me beside the changing tide, and on high mountains mantled with snow and in verdant valleys below — friends who have hiked with me along the highways of happiness and hope, who have meandered with me in meadows and marketplaces and walked in winding ways in the wilderness of difficult days. For all of these precious pilgrims on the path, I am most grateful.

I am thankful to JoAnn Beeson for her typing the manuscript and her suggestions about content and format. I appreciate the assistance that Nicola M. Tauraso has given concerning the details of publication.

I am grateful to you who now journey with me as you walk through the leaves and over the paths of print contained herein. In so doing, you have gifted me with a part of your life.

Strolls
Along the Seaside and Into the Forest

God Thoughts

The mystery of God is one of the clearest of His revelations. In His veiledness God unveils Himself. This unveiling through mystery has important implications for our knowing God. It means that we cannot be searching for God with preconceived ideas of who God is. To do this is to "staticize" our experience of His ever-newness to us. To live in the mystery of God is to know that the ages of sages are simply stages in the parting of the veil. Thus we live according to highest probabilities rather than in the frustrating fragilities of the absolute certainty of knowing it all. God's mystery says that in history there will never be the demise of surprise for the cosmic kaleidoscope constantly turns and makes mosaics of meaning within the mystery. To live in the mystery of God creates that humility which brings tranquility to mind and spirit. To so live also brings responsibility and makes conscious our conscience. The mystery of God makes clear to us that we do not comprehend Him but that He apprehends us and loves us forever.

The love of God is the source and goal of our being. To receive Divine Love is to be extinguished; to reflect Divine Love is to give eternal light. To receive God's love is to pass away; to share God's love is to endure forever. God's love is the genesis of all growth and change for His love ever calls us to leave the lesser for the greater to go on and on in perpetual discovery of His grandeur, glory and grace. To totally love God is to perform every act as a sacrament with no concern for or expectation of results. To experience God's love is to experience the love for ourselves, for it is God's love for us that is the reason for us to love ourselves. We love ourselves only for God and we love each other for the same reason. Perfect love is God in the depths of our being meeting God who comes to us. In this perfect love, this perfect communion, we know that all creation is nothing other than love.

To love God is to serve Him, to serve Him with no expectation of wages, to serve Him not for fear of hell nor desire of heaven, but to serve Him for Himself alone. To serve God is to self-divest so that He may Self-invest. It is to one-point our lives so that our creed and deed agree with the seed of God within us. To rightly serve God is not just to act from facile fact, but to trust in the "must" of His will and word; it is to rejoice in the choice He continually places before our faces and to gratefully expand and extend the whole of our being so that there can be the freeing of those found bound. To serve God is to move from tedium to *Te Deum*.

To be perfectly centered in God is not odd nor oblivion. For it is only when we are in the center of God's eye that we can be and say "I." It is then that the whole creation joins in the elation and celebration of our elevation to the Father's throne.

Blessing, honor, glory and power be unto Him!

God's Name

Why do we rail, flail, assail
Those who give God other names?
Why not let God's love prevail
And stop playing games
With words,
Which like birds,
Are so elusive,
So inconclusive.

For God is in all words, all sound,
Yet beyond them, too;
By Him we are found
To be true
When we are seeing
His being
In all fine expressions,
In all kinds of persons.

Living for God

One lesson of life you should know,
Is to do all things for God,
And not care about the blow,
Of those who may think you odd.

For God is our greatest Lover,
Source of life that never ends,
In living for Him we discover,
The joy for which all life tends.

Dialogue With Diety

I said –

Thee, O God, I would see
In depth and height,
Darkness and light,
Through the veil of mystery.

God said –

If my being you would realize,
You must do more than open your eyes.
Set your heart to burning,
Your soul to yearning,
Your whole life turning
To me.
Flee
From your fantasy
Of unreality
And be
In me.

The Real Presence

Much of our deliberation,
Is to find the Creator in His creation,
But ultimately,
We must come to see,
That God's absence,
Is His real presence,
In His creativity.

Sexuality and Spirituality

"Then God said, 'Let us make man in our image, after our likeness; and let them have dominion over the fish of the sea, and over the birds of the air, and over the cattle, and over all the earth, and over every creeping thing that creeps upon the earth.' So God created man in his own image, in the image of God he created him; male and female he created them."

This terse verse is one of the most significant in all of Scripture. For here is made clear the inseparable relationship between our spirituality and our sexuality. The Holy Breath that creates is also the Word that designates our divine destiny (spirituality) and our human proclivity for creativity and harmony (sexuality). It is the interaction between our spirituality and sexuality that greatly determines the modality of our ways, the joy of our plays and the fruitfulness of our days.

Creation is the result of God's love. Spiritual love and sexual love are creative and native to the human self. When together these loves prevail, the veil between heaven and earth is parted and there is started the journey from sod to God. Expressed mutuality of spirituality and sexuality brings forth new heavens and new earths in the totality of our own universes.

Both spirituality and sexuality are universals in humanity and thus point to the vanity of claiming superiority by virtue of a more beautiful or a better individuality. The marriage of spirituality and sexuality moves us beyond the confining and conflicting culture of comparison which breeds and feeds envy.

Our spirituality causes us to contemplate our ultimate fate. Our sexuality stirs us to relate to a mate. Both tend toward union — one with the divine, the other with a person, and when spirituality and sexuality intertwine, we experience that beautiful communion with God, another and self.

Spirituality and sexuality speak of duality — Creator and creature, male and female. When spirituality and sexuality are blended, then is ended the dualities of each and we reach that union for which we all yearn. In one sense, sexuality is what we are; spirituality is what we can become. The merging of the two in our acting and thinking prevents us from shrinking from life and gives strength and hope in our present situation and joy and peace for future liberation.

Man's love for woman and woman's love for man form a beautiful span to the love of God. Conversely, our intense love for God is the divining rod for finding that sweet water of human love.

To fully experience our sexuality is to experience our selfhood and to experience our Godhood for we are made in his image. Our sexuality informs our spirituality and our spirituality fulfills our sexuality.

Spirituality and sexuality express similar needs which are the seeds for growth and fruition of selfhood — patience and peace, tenderness and gentleness, discipline and self-control, acceptance and understanding, sensitivity and responsibility.

Sexual love coupled with spiritual love helps one toward self-integration which is the demonstration of the intention of creation. For when our beings are integrated, we are emancipated from the slavery of separation and free to enter into full relation with our Creator.

The unique peak sexual experience between female and male is the finding of that Holy Grail offered to us by the Lord of life.

The source and goal of our spiritual and sexual self are also the same. Each comes from the breath and touch of God, each ascends from its life upon sod to the heights above where the God of love receives with joy or sorrow the fruits of our yesterday, today and tomorrow on earth.

I Love You

I love you,
Not because I can use you,
Nor fuse you
Into the mold of my life;
Not because I need your caress
In my time of stress
And strife.

I love you,
Not because you love me
And set me free
From loneliness;
Not because my rough places
Need the embraces
Of your tenderness.

I love you,
Not for your beauty
Nor for your duty
Each day;
Not for the gladness
Nor for the sadness
You portray.

I love you,
Not for the words you say
Nor for the prayers you pray
For me;
Not for the gifts you bring
Nor for the songs you sing
Of charity.

I love you,
Simply because -
You are you.

In Thee

In thee
I see
Eternity.

In your presence,
I touch the essence
Of life.

In your glance,
I advance
From weakness
To strength.

In your nod,
God
Speaks to me.

The Cosmic Connection

The quest for wholeness is often pursued through psychological processes and perspectives. Another important approach to wholeness is the cosmic connection.

As one begins to consider and contemplate the cosmos, there emerges, in some mysterious way, an awareness of a unifying force that holds all together — the soul of the whole. This awareness helps lead one to a faith that speaks of the kinship of all — a kinship that includes all that ever was and ever will be, not just a kinship in our present earth experience.

The realization in one's life of the soul of the whole is also to know that nothing is without meaning and purpose. The movement of the stars and planets has purpose. The joyful dramas and the tearful tragedies of one's innermost life do not happen in vain, even when they are played out in secret, unrecorded and uncelebrated. Meaning is written in the stars and also in the scars of the human heart.

The universe is the Creator's subtle discourse addressed to all parts and beings of His creation. In the cosmic perspective, wholeness is more than the sum of the parts; it is the hum of the parts to the voice vibrations of the Eternal Word which continually calls His creation to full and perfect harmony.

For us to experience a kinship with all that was, is and is to be, to know that meaning and purpose, even though cradled in mystery, is inherent in both microcosmic and macrocosmic happenings, and to feel and hear — far or near — the melodies of the seas of God's love — below or above — all of these move us toward a wholeness that we have probably not even imagined possible.

To connect oneself to this cosmic consciousness causes new expressions and experiences of love. Now love is consciousness continually striving to be aware of and responsive to Divine Consciousness; concern for the well being of all creation; consecration to the Supreme Lover and creation of value for all that receives love given. In the cosmic connection, love is uncalculated and incalculable energy that goes out of oneself to set in motion forces that bring wholeness to that which is loved. Love is the power that creates, moves, holds together and gives meaning to the universe — for God is Love. Love is the vision of God in all things and of all things in God.

The path to wholeness is the way of love — love of God, neighbor, self and the universe. Our wholeness is the fullness of our love every moment. Love is the necessary nowness of being. Creation is an act of love and it is perpetual. At each moment our existence is God's love for us. We are because love is.

Would we know the meaning of wholeness, would we be whole? Then love now — love God now, love one another now, love self now, love all of life now. The heavens will rejoice, the stars will dance with you and you will be whole.

Far Vision

To reach out farther into the sky,
And with its mysteries cope,
Man has stretched the strength of his eye,
With the powerful telescope.

But for all the wonders telescopes yield,
As they search the heavens above,
None can compare with the heaven revealed,
Through tears in the eyes of love.

The Sky and I
Or
Out Is In

Scientists have many a calculation,
To tell us about the star,
My simple little revelation –
The light is not at all far.

The fact of the matter is simply this,
That each star is God's creation,
Between star and me there's no great abyss,
But the closest substantial relation.

The star is alive with God's energy,
I, too, am sustained by this motion,
Both star and I are alive and free,
Each a part of the divine ocean.

And so when I gaze into the sky,
Far out into infinity,
Then it is I know that I,
Am seeing a part of me.

Balance

One of the most important realities in all of creation is that of balance. Balance is essential in the world of nature. The movement of planets and atoms in their orbit, the passing of days and nights, seasons, sun and rain, the chemistry and metabolism in the bodies of living beings all manifest the necessity of balance for life. One of the great questions of modern times — that of ecology — is primarily a question of balance.

The worlds of science and technology, of art and music are based on balance. Mighty machinery, skyscrapers, delicate instruments and medicine; water, air and land transportation, as well as the soul-enriching creations of art and music, demand balance for proper functioning and beauty.

Human societies need balance for survival. Civilizations and cultures grow and prosper as the balance between supply and demand is maintained, as the political structure finds balance between various government functions and as freedom is balanced with responsibility.

One aspect of balance so important for a meaningful and abundant life in individuals is the balance between the head and the heart. The accumulated scientific and technological achievements of our society are positive proof of the power and possibilities of the human mind. Comfort, convenience and conquest constitute the fruits of the insatiable intellect. Reason reigns and ranges over many regions of our lives. But in its reign, reason often rains, bringing floods of facts and figures that confuse and confound, causing us to be adrift on the seas of life. These seas, whipped by the winds of the "wise," sometimes form whirlpools that begin to suck us into the dark abyss.

It is in the midst of this at-seaness, of this undertow of uncertainty and this spiraling down that love becomes a harbor of hope and a port of promise. Love is the dove bearing the olive branch from the sought-for shore and the sign of precious peace. The movement of the heart propels us through the scattered shoals and wild waves to higher ground where altitudes afford new attitudes. As the wind and waves of reason become more calm under the gentle caress of love, balance becomes ours.

Positioned in this balance, the land on which we stand begins to blossom and bless. Love becomes the floodgate that now allows the inland waters of the intellect to flow to arid wastelands of our lives. Love becomes the natural filter through which the streams of reason flow toward our thirst for truth. The finger of God, who is love, stirs the pools of our mind so that they become oasis for the thirsty caravan of humanity.

Then as the shadows bring their balm of coolness and calm and as the silent stars climb the ancient sky, the head and the heart, finding their perfect balance in our being, share their rest together. And we are at peace.

As Above — So Within

When storm and tempest rage without,
And darkness covers the land,
When angry men scream and shout
With weapons in their hand,
When life lays at your door,
Pain, suffering, tragedy,
Or loneliness brings its store,
Of sorrow and futility,
Then go within and find that calm,
That joy and hope and love,
And you will know that healing balm,
That comes from heaven above.

Relationships

Our relationships with other persons, whether near to us or far, become an important polestar which helps to guide us through the seas of life. Through another we discover new aspects of ourselves. Interdependence breaks down the fence of perilous pride. Involvement with humanity is not vanity, but the mark of sanity, for we are all part of the whole. Together we grow, together we know that life cannot be lived alone.

What can we do to renew life with others? We can try to see with the same eye, to hear with the same ear. The more that we put ourselves in another's place, walk with their pace, experience what others face, then we begin to truly know and flow with them.

Giving is another way of living in harmony with humanity. But giving, from the very start, must come from the heart. Noble and caring ideals can be the wheels which bear the chariots of charity that carry us to others in need, who then feed us.

We are to also know that to disagree with another is not to smother friendship, but rather to disagree is to free us from conformity and allow us (and the other) to uniquely be oneself. We often learn the most not from those who boast about us, but from those who fuss with us. Those who have different views offer us new clues to truth.

To recognize and greet the Spirit in the heart of each is to reach a depth of understanding, love and appreciation that bring joy, peace and emancipation from conflict and crazy competition. We do this by loving God first and it is then that our thirst for communion and communication with another is assuaged.

The uniqueness of each human being provides perspectives for seeing both partialities and totalities in life.

When we acquaint ourselves with differences in others, we remove the covers that keep us from expressing our own uniqueness.

As we travel our way, we are not to "lay our trip" on others. We simply share our experience and offer no defense for it, regarding it as a gift which another may lift to the light of his or her own experience and then receive or reject what we have given.

To admit that we do not know all is a humble call to others to come and share life together.

In summary, we see that we live with others in community which at times brings perplexity and creates difficulty. This need not be if our sensitivity to others is serious and sincere. When our ideals are high and when we are at center, we need not shy from others nor fail to enter their spaces, but see them as sisters and brothers who also wish to move out of the traces that hold them back. Good relationships blossom and bloom when there is room in our hearts and minds for other kinds of ideas and life styles. To touch another's soul is to begin to relate to the whole of that person. Listening to another who is "at odds" can pop the pods of our pride, prejudices and narrowness, and enable us to press fearlessly forward into new or deeper relationships. To respect the uniqueness of each is to reach out in gratitude to another. Our humility can often be the best key to good relationships.

So, our journeys and voyages through this life need not be filled with storm and strife. If we will hear and heed and act out in deed the mandate of the Master to love God and self, then we can love others and walk with them hand in hand to the Promised Land.

The Fire of Love

Who are you, who am I?
Where is God, why must we die?
What is truth, what is peace?
When will wars and hatred cease?

Day by day more questions come,
Yet our eager lips stay dumb,
For we have not yet learn'd how,
To let our minds to our hearts bow.

Our minds in darkness lie entombed,
Until our lives are all consumed,
By the fire of love.

Sacrament

The vision by which I now am led,
The vision I'm always seeing,
Is to share with you the heavenly bread,
Of my own self-being.

This is the vision that all must see,
If there's to be an end to strife,
The vision that so perfectly,
Shows the true sacrament of life.

A Christian Introspection

In a time when many voices are calling us to make choices for candidates, products or ideologies, we often find ourselves in confusion, and sometimes in delusion. We look for clarification through our own identification. Who are we and what are we called to do?

As we look backward to our beginnings, we see ourselves as children of God created in his image (we know who we are when we know whose we are), carriers of the Christ-consciousness, challengers to the church and the world to boldly move out to new frontiers of faith and freedom.

The future also influences our present and continually adds its comment to the conversation of the now moment. We all live in the context of the not-yetness which, like the wetness of morning dew, covers the landscape of life now. We live lives that are unfulfilled — lives that have not yet thrilled to all that is possible for us. Convergences of philosophies, religions, cultures, races, political and economic systems are future possibilities that are beginning to manifest now. Each of these mergings will bring new drama and trauma and radical change which can rearrange, even derange, our mental and spiritual balance. We participate in convergences now by pointing to positive possibilities and by reinforcing faith to make the transitions. We become convergence catalysts as each sifts out fear of the unknown and enthrones trust in God in the center of one's being.

The seemingly limitless power that persons presently possess or pursue presages perilous passages for pilgrims along the path. Catastrophes, spawned from the wombs of fatalistic fantasies, loom even more frequent on the horizon of humanity. We are thus challenged to be discoverers and bearers of new power possibilities of the spirit which can guide and control other powers that threaten life.

Convergences and catastrophes call for new concepts and experiences of community, new expressions of unity for humanity — now a necessity if we are to continue to be. The future looks back to us in the present and with a great intent urges us to be preservers, promoters and prophets for a community that seeks first to know, love and serve God.

Jesus said that the kingdom of God is within. Every quest for identity involves an inner journey. So we are explorers and miners descending to the cavernous depths of the soul for the gems of goodness. We are surgeons probing the deep chambers of the heart to touch the heart of God. We are divers plunging through the dark waters of the mind to reach the pearl of great price — the truth. These endeavors involve risk, ridicule, resentment, rejection and radical changes in attitudes, beliefs and behavior. Life's precious passages always involve pain but the effort is never in vain.

So the journey inward indicates who we are. We are frontiersmen who do not fear the fickle finger of fellowmen who point with judgement and resentment. We are ones who hunger and thirst for the kingdom of God within ourselves and who strive to share that kingdom with others when we find it. Each who embarks on the journey inward becomes a disciplinarian preparing for the burdens and blessings of the future. We are gardeners of the soil of the soul and guardians of the fortress of freedom — freedom for each person to make his or her own spiritual pilgrimage.

We start near to go far. As we penetrate our inner spaces, we find ourselves engaged in gentle embraces with the world around us. We become selves not by remaining on shelves of isolation, but by entering into conversation and relation with others. We understand who we are by understanding who our fellow humans are, and we understand who others are when we stand under, with, for and among them sharing joys, sorrows, pleasures, pains, successes, failures, hopes and despairs. The real profanity within humanity is not dirty language but a shutting out of persons, whatever their age, from the circle of life.

While recognizing diversity and differences, we strive to break down the walls and fences that divide and diminish persons. We are a fellowship that aims to affirm the worthship of all persons, to facilitate the unity of humanity at the deepest level where all are one. In our outward reach, we are challenged to be builders of homes of harmony, hospitality, hope and happiness; healers for the hurts of humanity; teachers and preachers to all creatures; pupils and students of all movements and events which come from the sum of God's creation.

We are weavers of robes to warm cold humanity; carpet makers for the weary and stone-bruised feet of persecuted pilgrims. We make ropes, not to bind, but ropes that help mankind find the means to freedom from the oceans of despair and from the quicksands of greedy grasping hands.

So who are we? We are each unique expressions of God's love, diviners of divinity, children of eternity, flowing in divergency, yet ebbing into unity. We are called to remember and to respect our roots and to always be cultivating our fruits. We are challenged to risk passage through the dark spaces so we may come to the world with embraces of light. We are bearers of hope with the message that we are blessed with a universe with which we can converse in myriad ways. We are lovers of life and our life is love. We are of God, and though we daily trod the sod, we know and ever try to show our ultimate destiny is that of divinity.

Meaning

O unique expression of God,
You ask what does life mean,
And again you fitfully trod,
Over the same old scene,
The no-man's land of doubt,
And you cry out and shout,
What does my life mean?

Be still, O soul, and hear,
That gentle voice inside,
Which dissipates your doubts and fear,
In which you so often hide,
That tells of your particularity,
And your unique responsibility,
To in God's love abide.

Divine Weaver

O Divine Weaver,
I offer you the threads of my life,
Weave them into a fabric of beauty,
To be seen by those who know only strife,
And see life only a difficult duty.

With Your love,
Make these threads warm,
So that they may comfort the old,
Give life to the forlorn,
Food and warmth to the hungry and cold.

Weave these threads so they are strong,
To rescue the little child,
When she becomes weak or goes wrong,
Or when she is reviled.

Life's Meaning

Does life have meaning or is our living simply gleaning the left-overs from harvested fields of others' lives? Is life worthwhile or is our life simply a cry and a smile in the midst of a few gains and many pains?

These are questions that many consider essential if one's potential for wholeness and wellness is to be realized. Purpose, meaning, validity and value of life are constantly set forth as important ways to handle strife and, with strong intent, find joyful and successful fulfillment. These questions are not to be denied, yet when answers are tried they are found wanting and the mystery of life keeps haunting our hearts.

The key answer about living is giving. After all is said and done, life is simply a gift in which we are not to sift pleasure and pain, sunshine and rain, loss or gain, but with a grateful heart accept every part of life that is given.

To receive life as a gift is to know not the drift of one's life, but to know the one true intent for which life is lent — that life be spent each moment in love. For the gift of life is the gift of love.

When we know and love the Lover, we discover life. To love the Giver of life is to no longer ask questions about life, for to love God answers all questions. In loving God we experience bliss even in the abyss, rapture in His capture of our will, great joy in the employ of His service and a knowing that needs no showing from the minds of men.

God, the Giver and Lover, does not smother mind nor reason, but leads us through each season of life so that we learn and mature from our own nature — within and without.

So in our questing for life's meaning by constantly screening, analyzing and synthesizing perceptions and evidence, conceptions and even nonsense, let us realize that the gift of life may be unwrapped by our minds but the gift itself is received by our heart.

Wishes For Your Life

May the beauty of this day
Find its unobstructed way
Into your life.

May those who come to you
Find their spirits anew
From your life.

May you find abundant living
From the fullness you are giving
Of your life.

A Lesson

Man thinks he's clever,
And thus can sever,
Himself from his destiny,
By sitting alone,
On a royal throne,
Of total liberty.

But man's a part,
Just like the hart,
Of God's totality,
And he must discover,
The plan of the Lover,
Is complementarity.

Why

Why do I run and hide from the rain,
That showers its love on me?
Why do I again and again,
Reject the wind's kisses so free?

Why do I not hear the voice of the lark,
As he sings to warm my heart?
Why do I not even embark,
On a voyage to see a tree's art?

Why do I pass by the rose's fragrance,
That's offered to me 'til it dies?
Why do I never even glance,
At the paintings of the skies?

Why am I so unaware,
Of the ways God touches me?
Why must I always be so spare,
In receiving love's bounty?

Science and Spirit

One of the oft-overlooked contributions of science today is the interesting way in which scientific and technological achievements point to the presence of the spiritual. Explorations into the macrocosm and microcosm take us farther and deeper into the realms of radical reality. The wonder of the many levels and the vastness of the range of depths in the interior of physical reality speak of a subtle spirituality. The immensity of things known, the immensely distant and beyond and the immensely near and within, the immensely large and immensely small — these all are a call to a new view of God. The excitement of the not-yet encountered, the dynamic dances between certainty and uncertainty, the undeviating determinacy and the probing probabilities, the confusing complexities and the satisfying simplicities are mysteries of the histories of the universes. The discoveries of science can move us to greater reliance on the world of the spirit. Science is helping us to better see that behind the visible is the Mind of the invisible.

By reflecting on the transcendent in nature, we are led beyond conjecture to the realization of our relation, our interdependence with the world around us. Even before birth, we are umbilical to earth. Through rocks and trees, plants and seas, through sun and stars, nights and days, we experience the awesome ways in which our lives are constantly touched by a presence which escapes our comprehension and control. When examining and encountering the natural world we also encounter ourselves.

The trips of the adepts into the depths of our minds bring new kinds of insights into the rituals and rites of religion. Psychological and parapsychological explorations and penetrations reveal exciting manifestations of the divine within. Analyses of personal crises within our lives help us to realize that not just in the skies but in the deeps of our consciousness there is the comfort and caress of a loving Creator.

The dependencies and contingencies which scientific methodologies uncover tell us of Another who causes us to be. We are neither self-originating nor self-sustaining; we are always draining energy from divinity. Our dependence on Deity enables us to be free to be. Dependence is the key to independence which opens the door to integrating interdependence with our fellow human beings.

Various branches of science note our incompleteness which is not so much a weakness as the persistent press for fulfillment. There is an open-endedness in our being that encourages possibilities for a future filled with power and perfection. Through inward pressures, recognition of potentials for growth, and through dissatisfaction with what we are — these pulls to a greater purpose are indicative of a greater Purposer.

The search of science for the "how" often facilitates the search of the spirit for the "why" and the "now." Science's successes help to remove the tresses that sometimes get in the spirit's eye and occlude the "why" of life. Meaningful living is not gleaningful living. Meaningful living is living at the heart of the harvest as a part of the great Harvester.

So the scientist says that the universe can be trusted and that it is not in a conspiracy against mankind. This affirmation of faith is for the spiritual person another confirmation of faith. It is faith in the wholeness and holiness of all that is. This faith proclaims that we put aside exclusionism in exchange for the reality of a total unity.

So science serves the spirit; spirit supports science. Together they bring us to God.

Cosmic Kaleidoscope
A View for the Third Eye

God –

Maker and shaper,
Of all the pieces,
Breaker and shaker,
Of cosmic caprices.

Artist of every single hue,
Source of the lights that burn,
Eye that watches every view,
Hand that makes every turn.

All that is falls into place,
Replacing despair with hope,
Cause, motion, time merge with space,
In the cosmic kaleidoscope.

Ode to an Electron

Whirling, swirling little mass,
How can I forbid thee pass,
Through my orbit day by day,
Lest myself I pass away.

From a Proton

Death

The democracy of death embraces all of us. Even before its actual arrival, death is an absent presence. To be aware of death and to try to understand its meaning, is to sharpen and intensify our awareness of life. Attitudes about death serve an important organizing principle in determining how one conducts himself in life. Facing death is facing self, and integrating the death concept into one's life helps to integrate oneself here and now.

There are many approaches to understanding the implications of the meaning of death and what follows.

What we commonly call death is dissolution of the flesh body and the removal of that body from our midst. To one on the spiritual path, death is this — but also much more than this. Death is a moment of unfolding and growth, a breaking out and moving beyond the time-space-motion continuum, a new face-to-faceness with other reality. *Psyche* (soul) now released from flesh has the opportunity to more freely relate to *pneuma* (spirit) from which it sprang. Death raises the curtain on the divine drama of psycho-pneumatics.

For one who has loved God while in the physical body, death is the movement of life forward by going backward to the will of original creativity. For one who has denied and defied God, death is the movement of life backward to the justice of original creativity. One who has affirmed God as father conceives of death as mother which gives birth to a new and glorious life.

The nature of the encounter with death and its aftermath depends on one's relationship to God, to his fellow man and to himself during his earthly pilgrimage. This truth has not only been proclaimed, prophesied and promised by persons in all ages and culture, but this truth is embedded in the very nature of being itself.

What about this nature of life following death? Ideas, dogmas and doctrines have abounded in all civilizations. Man has sought answers through the tenets of his religious faith, through philosophical theses, through many kinds of sensory and extrasensory phenomena and simply through going deep within himself to feel some intimations and explanations of immortality.

Life after death — like life before death — is growth. The on-going process of life changes form and substance, but the integrity of purpose and meaning continues the same. Life before and after death can be distinguished, but not separated. The essence of life, the soul, continues to be called to accountability and challenged to natural unfoldment. Personality, personal identity, familiar concepts and constructs of the being are maintained. Personal relationship and communication are possible with those in the physical body as well as with those who are not.

The on-going life enters into our time-space-motion categories, but also transcends them. Awareness of the unobstructedness, of the oneness of the universe, becomes more acute. More possibilities for unimaginable creativity are present. New opportunities for repentance and reconciliation are made available. Life at any level, at any time, becomes its own redeemer when that life allows itself it be taken fully into the realm of the love of its Creator. Consciousness continues and is expanded, sharpened and challenged. Responsibility and choice, activities of the will, become extremely important.

To be born is to be given a gift. To experience death is also to be given a gift. The gift is the same in each case — life. The giver is the same — God. Cherish and be good to your gift and ever be grateful to the Gift Giver.

Immortality

Everywhere we see,
Glimpses of immortality,
If we but gaze,
Beyond the glaze,
Of partiality.

The root of all being,
Goes deep beyond the seeing,
Of bits and pieces,
And tedious theses.

Immortality,
Is breaking free,
Of partiality,
And nesting, questing, jesting,
In the creativity,
Of unity,
O God,
With Thee.

Teacher Death

Think not of death as final enemy,
Ever seeking to conquer you in strife,
But know death is striving to help you see,
The meaning of your present precious life.

Cradled

The door to the future is seldom open,
We know not what lies ahead,
The secret of time's womb is not broken,
Uncertain is one's tread.

But uncertainty, mystery, obscurity,
In the flux of the sifting sands,
Have no fearful grip on me,
When I know,
In life's flow,
Every phase,
Of my days,
Is cradled in God's hands.

Fruits of the Spirit

An important spiritual truth oft noted and quoted for its universal and clear message is "by their fruits you shall know them." This adage applies to every age in the history of mankind as well as to one's personal history. The quality of our fruits reflects the depths of our roots in the soil of the Spirit. In our journey through life we search for ways through the strife which often confuses and controls our behavior. The fruits of the spirit provide a guide through the maze and haze of programmed propaganda which constantly tries to prioritize our lives.

The first fruit of the spirit is love — of God, neighbor and self. Love fulfills the law (God's laws are God's loves), is balm for the raw emotions and, like mighty oceans, brings up treasures from the deep to both share and keep. A loving heart is the truest wisdom and where perfect love is, fear has no kingdom. The language of love is understood by all and the hand of love lifts us when we fall. Love, like a precious ointment, blesses and beautifies the vessel in which it is stored as well as the object on which it is poured. Like the sun to the earth, love nutures, heals and enlightens. Love understands and waits with outstretched hands at the gates — even the gates of hell.

The fruit of joyfulness is the healing caress for the pain of sadness. Joy is the many-spoked wheel within from which spin the lights of laughter, the sounds of humor, the scent of contentment. Joy is the heart's singing and the soul's winging to heights of happiness. Gladness prolongs life, dissipates strife within and without and is strength for the weak. Joy unites — a merry heart knows no age and all smile in the same language.

The fruit of peace comes from the surcease of conflict within. We cannot bring flowers in our hands if our hearts are volcanoes or if we are caught in the throes of anger. We know perfect peace when we enter the center of the heart of God and dwell therein. To know peace on earth is to be at peace with heaven. The peace that passes all understanding comes not by demanding, but surrendering our wills to God.

Patience is the fruit of positive, persistent and purposeful power. Patience sees with the eyes of faith beyond the temporal to the eternal. For the patient person, affliction does not become an addiction but a spiritual promotion. They who wait patiently upon the Lord are not bored, but renew their strength and know that it is not the length of days but the quality that sets them free. Patience knows God's delays are not God's denials. The tears and pains of patience are the rains which wash our eyes so we become more wise. Patience looks up and sees the sun while standing in the mud. Patience raises the eyebrows and not the roof.

The fruit of gentleness grows from the root of tenderness. Gentleness is the soft caress of word and deed on hurting humanity; the warm compress on the wounds wrought by piercing profanity. Gentleness is the hand of love and wisdom leading the child through the foreboding forests of fear and failure. Gentle is the one who stops a heart from breaking, who eases a pain the aching, who helps in the making of peace on earth.

Goodness is another fruit of the spirit that derives from Godness. Goodness and truth go hand in hand. Goodness is a light that dispels the darkness of disappointment, disgrace and despair. When goodness is shared, it is paired with hope and lives are changed. To be good is to bring food to those who hunger of body, mind and spirit.

The fruits of faith are found far and wide, without, within and by our side. Faith grows in the valley, affirms the urchins in the alley, leads a sally against doubt and offers a shout of encouragement for those who falter along the way. The oasis of faith is not reached by the caravan of the mind, but by trust in the "must" of God's word and will. Faith fills the future with light, dispelling the gloom of futile fear. Firm faith in the Father dissipates fear of Adam or the atom.

The fruit of kindness is sweet for the one who gives and for the one who receives. Kindness removes the blindness of our egocentricity and, like electricity, lights our homes (home is where the heart is) and the homes of others. To be kind is to find the pearl of great price. Kindness is the dress of love and, as a fruit of the spirit, one cannot get rid of it. When kindness is expressed to another, it returns to hover over us like an angel of light ready to renew our life.

The fruit of self-control is not a troll to keep us from crossing the bridges of life. Self-control is the fruit that helps us root in the ground of respect and right. It is the discerning in our yearning, the reining of our straining, the containing of our fire of desire — moderation of the escalation of excessive emotion. Self-control is to determine our own course and not let the force of another take charge of our life.

These are some of the fruits of life. How does your orchard grow?

Preparing the Soil

Plough deep, O God, the soil of my soul,
With Your love-tempered plough,
That when falls the seed,
Of deepest need,
I may say, "Lord, I'm ready now."

Aware

To be aware,
Is not to stare,
Nor glare,
At the world,
In its nakedness or garb.

To be aware,
Is not to declare,
That you know,
The chemistry of snow,
Or the reason for the rose's barb.

To be aware,
Is not to compare,
And then in the choice,
To rejoice,
That you've succeeded,
And weeded,
Out the wrong.

To be aware,
Is to share,
Your being,
Thus freeing,
Soul,
From the dark hole,
Of selfish care,
That makes you,
Unaware.

Truth

The beginning of the journey toward liberty is to know that truth is not composed nor imposed by others from without with sword, pen or shout, but that truth lies within our own being waiting for its freeing. Truth is within our own center and as others enter our heart and mind, we begin to find the truth in us stirs to meet the guest who is often on the same quest. These guests that come to us are many and we are not to bar any if our search for truth is sincere.

Science comes to our door with ever more revelations and helps to remove the hesitations on our journey to the light. Whether of sky, sea or earth, the persistency of scientific methodology and technology continues to give birth to truth that has long lain in the womb of wisdom. The scientist is a welcome guest on the path to truth.

Nature, in all of her beauty and serendipity, is also a party to our understanding of reality. Desert and sea, mountains and valley, bird, beast and insect all reflect light from the bright countenance of truth. As we open our heart's door to nature's store of gifts, we find truth emerging and ever urging us to accept more.

For many, art is the heart of truth. Colors and forms become the dorms in which truth dwells. Portraying history in event, person and place, the artist enables us to trace the sources and courses of life. Responding to the promptings from within, the artist sees into the mysteries of the future. His or her many-colored strokes become the spokes on the wheel that carries us forward on the journey to authenticity.

Music oft moves heart and soul toward the goal of truth. The multiplicities of harmonies and melodies reveal the countless possibilities which abound in the universe of sound. Various musical vibrations from all nations bring the ring of truth. The music we hear with ear brings us near to the Conductor of the symphony of life. In His presence we gain a new sense of truth.

Sometimes at our heart's door, faith appears as a waif which we choose to ignore. But it is this often unkempt child that pleads for us to hear and leads us from the fear of rejection to a new direction to truth. When we receive faith in our dwelling place, we begin to face the cosmos within and without and move beyond doubt.

Hope knocks at our door and invites us to explore the frontiers of truth in the not-yetness of life. From wells deep, hope trys to keep our gardens of life alive. Hope looks ahead to unseen horizons and calls us to orisons for truth which may be manifested on this plane.

Now love comes to our home to tell us of truth. As we open the door of our heart and soul to love's energies, mysteries of truth are unveiled. Love as the root of our being brings forth the fruit of our seeing truth anew. For love is not blind, but is rather the kind and gentle gift of God that opens eyes, hearts and minds so that we experience totalities rather than partialities. Love is the quest that brings peace and rest to confused minds and troubled hearts and it is in this rest that the clarity of veracity becomes ours. Ultimately truth can only be known when love is enthroned in our being. For God, the Source of all truth, is love. We, being made in God's image, are love, and when we perfectly love, we not only know the truth, but we are truth.

The ways to truth are manifold, but the fullness of truth comes when we hold all creation in our arms of love and when we allow ourselves to be held by the Creator within, below and above.

Be True

Life calls us to be true in thought,
In word and in our deed,
Life shows the battle must be fought,
With the sower of falsehood's seed.

For truth cannot be cast aside,
Or buried in a hole,
Truth cannot be denied,
For it is life to the soul.

Always seek to be true,
Weed out the falsity,
Life's garden will then yield for you,
The blossoms of liberty.

Responsibility

As I look at the world and deplore the destruction,
That around me does constantly abound,
I seldom pause to ask the question,
Why have I not made a good sound.

A sound to offer my head, hand and heart,
To those on destruction bent,
A sound that can really sincerely impart,
A message of wholesome intent.

To rant and rave at those who tear down,
And not love within my own soul,
Is to in the depths of deception drown,
To deny I'm a part of the whole.

The Practice and Primacy of Prayer

The practice of prayer is primary for the pilgrim on the path. For prayer is soul energy turning to its life source for growth and power and communion. It is a gentle, spiritual movement that brings about a face-to-faceness of human soul with Divine Spirit. Prayer is soul energy yearning to express its great gratitude to God for being and yearning to declare its dependence on God. Prayer is soul energy burning — it is selfhood aflame — and seeking to unite with the Eternal Fire of Love.

Prayer is one-ing with God, a concrete expression of one's particular participation in the cosmic continuum. Prayer is a honing of awareness of our lostness. It is a homing which cancels our aimlessness and homelessness and removes us from ravages of restless refugeeism. Prayer is a true expression of who we are. We make ourselves what we are by the way we address God. Prayer thus becomes not only a remembering of what we have been, but also an awareness of what we now are and what we can be. It is a simultaneous integrating and restructuring activity of the soul. Prayer is asking oneself to give an account of self in order to face life and confess who one really is. It is not being afraid to be human.

But prayer is also a forgetting of self which is a form of freedom and a remembering of God which is a form of meeting. Prayer is the stirring of cosmic consciousness — an effort to get out of our guarded ghettos and expand our beings, and to lead the active life in accordance with the inherent pattern of the universe.

Mystical prayer, i.e., prayer that incorporates much silence, solitude, contemplation, is the exposing of self to the promptings of God and to the light of His truth that purifies and illumines faith. It is the quiet surrender and incubation period of the soul during which new confidences, trusts, hopes and peace are born. Mystical prayer is the mind's spiraling down to the core of one's being, a transfer of energy in the conscious mind to a deeper level where transformation of being takes place by cleansing, gathering and unifying one's motives. It is a purification of the unconscious.

Mystical prayer helps to better root one in the common ground of humanity and to see one's concern for another in terms of ultimate concern. It is being with another in depth. It is recognizing the reality of humanity not as an "it" but as a "thou." This increases willingness to trust others, to better identify with others and to have a sense of universal belonging.

Prayer

Prayer is
The sally of the soul,
Into God's mystery,
The rally of the whole,
Self for integrity.

Vision

The vision of eternity,
A trip to celestial lands,
Sometimes comes on bended knee,
And with gently folded hands.

Prayer for Light

God,
From birth,
Thou hast made me more than clod,
Of earth.

But,
So often I am found,
In the rut,
Bound, to the ground.

O effulgent deity,
Shine from above,
Let me transparent be,
To reveal Thy love.

O Lord, most kind,
Wipe clean my soul,
Fix, focus, the mirror of my mind,
To reflect Thee, my source, my goal.

Alleviating Anxiety

Since the beginning of civilization, human society has experienced anxiety. As human life becomes more complex, anxieties more and more vex body, mind and spirit. An example is the production of hundreds of medicines for the reduction of pain and strain. This is not a very merry commentary on the human situation.

Anxieties are expressed in many ways and intensities. Some anxieties are new to our day; others have held sway since the beginning of human history. Three of the latter are the anxieties about death, meaninglessness and guilt. The anxiety about death is that life as we know it now will someday end with our last breath. The anxiety of meaninglessness is that life is often seen as an aimless wondering and wandering in a wanton wilderness. The anxiety of guilt involves one's concern about proper relationships to God, others and self.

Faith in life after death has given new life and breath to many. The fear of dying gives way to relying on the wisdom of God whose Word proclaims that man is not confined or condemned to the sod, but that his destiny is eternity. Dissipating the death anxiety permits us to be free, to live more abundantly here and now. New perspectives on death and life reduce strife caused by the passing of loved ones and offer hope for one's own future.

Prayer and meditation become man's mediation for meaning. History shows that man thrashes in the throes of aimlessness when he charts his course without consulting or relating to life's source. Prayer and meditation are more than a gleaning for meaning. They are the quest for the harvest of abundance and the continuance of intentional living. The anxiety of meaninglessness is always made less when one turns to and yearns for his Maker.

The anxiety of guilt as a fact of the human situation may be denied by some. But the nature of man is that in this life's span, his life is not always pure. However, there is a cure. One need not live in the valleys of despair because he is not always fair to another; nor need one remain in a dungeon of depression because of a sometime suppression of a fellow human. Healing is always at hand if one can feel and understand the love and mercy of God.

The message of faith, hope and love is that these anxieties need not be. For if one can live in God through prayer and through healing share one's life with others, if one can know the flow of life in God who is forever, then no force — however clever — can move one to be undone by anxiety. If God is our center, then we shall enter his Kingdom right now and find ways to bring others, our sisters and brothers.

The Search

Within, without, we seek to know,
The reasons for our pain and woe,
At times the answer's from above,
And sometimes from an absent love;
Often the answer's nowhere.

Unsettled, anxious, beset with fears,
Our smiles so often turn to tears,
Yet always comes a brighter day,
When all our tears are wiped away.

When doubt, despair and dread prevail,
And we cry out to no avail,
Pause, pray, and give thanks to the Lord,
That this sharp, severing sword,
That pierces mind and soul,
Can also make us whole.

And thank God too,
That even you,
Despite your pain,
Can still obtain,
His love –
And mine.

Live Now

Live –
Draw deeply the breath of life,
Live now,
Do not worry about the strife,
Or how,
You will meet tomorrow,
Or deal with sorrow.

For as you live this moment,
Gratefully, fully, freely,
Then you will be sent,
The wisdom and capacity,
To meet the day,
In an unexpected way.

Love

To love is the greatest experience in life. Therefore, it is important to talk about love, to feel it, treasure it, give and receive it. Love is divine energy, that all-embracing activity that unites and enriches life, that binds beings without diminishing or destroying the beings involved. Love, at its best, is a delicate balance of unifying and separating, of binding and freeing, of integrating and maintaining identity. This balance is affected significantly by spaces in love.

1. *Secret space*. Every soul has its secret space. This secret space is a basic component of life because it helps to define one's uniqueness and singularity. A person is a person to a great extent as he has a secret space that is not shared with anyone else. In a love relationship the lover respects this space in the beloved because he realizes that here is where the beloved's self finds its ultimate meaning and mightiest motivation for life and love. To break into this spiritual privacy is to invade the core of his being. Paradoxically, the lover penetrates the secret space of the beloved by allowing him to maintain that space. In so doing, the lover goes deeper into his own secret space and finds that which is the source and meaning of the secret space of all souls. When one gets in touch with his own secret space, then he can begin to reach his beloved. The outward and inward reach toward the beloved depends greatly on the strength and integrity of the downward reach within the lover — a downward reach, the culmination of which raises love to its greatest heights.

2. *Listening*. Listening is a space that love requires. Listening in love is giving another the maximum of attention with a minimum of intention. Attention facilitates the creative process. Listening is an effort toward comprehending without apprehending the beloved's

consciousness. It is accepting one as he is and thereby allowing new discoveries to happen for both. Listening permits more room for the beloved to express his freedom and gives truth more time and space to grow. The lover who listens much forms a silent space to grow within his own being where delicate discernments, often blurred by dialogue, are made. It is then that hidden communion and increased awareness of the divine dimensions of love can better take place. Listening is a harvesting of the beloved's sowing which allows a mutual sharing of God's fruit.

3. *Detachment*. Detachment is a spacing of self from one's ego in order to move closer to the beloved. Detachment allows the aim of true love — the good of the beloved — to better be realized. Detachment enables the light of truth to shine forth and to remove the blindness which ego always brings to the love relation. Detachment permits reciprocation of love at its best because it forces the love relationship to locate its source beyond the individual egos and allows the mutual good of each to be joined together. Detachment permits other components of the love relation — respect, honesty, temperance, justice — to operate more fully. It enables one to better love God in the other.

4. *Solitude*. Loneliness is often the result of one's not being alone enough. Love needs solitude which is more than just physical separation from others. The lover needs the stillness and silence of sincere solitude in order to develop the goodness that is his own, to be with himself to learn to love himself. Pure interior solitude ultimately centers on God and here it is that one finds the proper priorities and perspectives for loving. Solitude participates in the solitariness of God. True solitude gathers in the wisdom, will and love of God and equips the lover for encounter with the world. Solitude teaches the lover to love another for what he is — not for

what he says. Solitude removes fear of engagement with persons or things because true solitude cleanses the soul so that the lover does not seek to possess. His will becomes an instrument for God's loving will which is directed toward creating new beings.

May you be blessed with many good spaces in living and loving.

Universalize Your Heart

Universalize your heart,
Let not just a part
Of creation experience your love.

Share with all the fullness of your soul,
Bring to the universe your whole
Being,
And thus participate in the freeing
Of creation from captivity,
To selfish particularity.

Night Journey

Moonlight on your path tonight,
And for your inn,
The sheltering shadow of my prayers,
And for your host,
My love.

The New Age

In the consciousness of many people today the New Age is front stage. Significant signs and developing designs are emerging and presenting a kaleidoscopic and often "utopic" picture of being and existence.

Creativity has always been an aspect of man's nature, but in our day human creativity is taking quantum leaps. The reasoned advances of science coupled with the changes of reliance on intuition and superstition, imagination and visualization, fantasy and heresy, cult and occult are all bringing forth constellations of new concepts, constructs, combinations; new words and symbols, new energies, ecstasies and enterprises that excite and incite, that captivate and activate, that dissipate and integrate bodies, minds and spirits. Creativity in the New Age — like creativity in any age — challenges us to choose responsibly for wholeness or irresponsibility for holocaust.

Convergence is an expression of the New Age. Convergence between East and West, between religious denominations, between races and places such as city and country (megalopolis), between the sciences and the resultant multi-disciplinary approaches to problem solving. In some cases these convergences are creating conflicts and confusion; in others, syntheses and serendipities. Convergence is bringing the emergence of new forms that call forth new norms of behavior.

Expanding *consciousness* is a dynamic of the New Age. Research on matter and energy is revealing the depths and complexity of consciousness. Study of the brain, the new science of psychopharmacology and the many types of psychotherapy are bringing us glimpses of the vast universe — beautiful and perverse — of the mind. Head shrinking is giving way to mind expanding as the way of understanding. A special aspect of the new consciousness is Christ-consciousness. This is appearing within and outside of the Christian Church. It is a more wholistic interpretation and experience of Jesus Christ — his mission, message and ministry.

Communication is an indication of the New Age. Whether through radioastronomy, ufology, telepathy or mystical ecstasy, communication is presenting new revelations and revolutions in human life. Communication with the macrocosm without and the microcosm within, with loved ones gone to another plane — these "touchings" are all helping to clean the dark pane through which we've so long looked.

Community is a sign of the New Age. Communes, ashrams, yoga and zen centers, meditation and wholistic health centers are some signs pointing to the hunger for meaningful human community in our day. Generally such communities are sincere strivings for growth toward wholeness. The best in New Age community is the full realization of humanity through the search for divinity.

Communion in the New Age is the quest for union with all creation. This is the reverence for life, the deterrence of strife. It is kinship and rightful relation replacing the sinship of frightful separation. Such communion is that form of worship that recognizes not only the worthship of the Creator but also of all that the Creator has made.

The New Age is here. Old forms are breaking, old foundations are shaking. Let us face the challenges that come with courage, consecrating ourselves by committing ourselves first and above all else to the One who gives us life and who is Lord over all the ages.

Mining

What will you take from the mines of life,
As you dig from morn 'til night?
Will it be the gravel of strife,
Or the gold of love so bright?

Illusion

The cause of so much strife and stress,
That harrass humanity,
Is the sharp urge to possess,
More of the Edenic tree.

But life is not to gain the tree,
To do so is to be regressed,
To have is not to be free,
To possess is to be possessed.

Spiritual Sensitivity and Maturity

Movement toward spiritual sensitivity and maturity happens in many ways. One is the manner in which we observe a person, place, thing or situation. If we look not just at, but look within and beyond, and if we observe with the thought that this is the first and last time we shall have this particular experience, then not only our eyes but also our skies — our higher consciousness and heart — are opened. This openness is a gentle caress for the spirit.

Spiritual sensitivity and maturity are increased through listening. To really listen is to want to hear and it is this wanting that lessens our own intention and increases our attention to what is occurring. It is extreme attention (glistening listening) that activates the creative faculty in both the listener and the one who is listened to. To listen with care allows one to share heights and depths and to have space to be — to be free.

To be open to new ideas, whatever their source or force, can be spiritually enriching. Often it is the most far-out concept that is our introduction to the adept, the strangest thing that will bring us to the "Ah, Ha!" experience, the word of the heretic that will prick our conscience, the weirdest thought that will cause us to be caught up into seventh heaven. To be open does not always indicate our readiness to agree, accept, adopt or supplicate. To be open means to recognize that in someone's eyes truth is seeking to emerge. This provides the occasion for the using of our gifts of discernment and choice-making, two of the most precious and sacred gifts we have.

Spiritual journeys, at least in this life, are made in the embrace of time and space. Though our destiny is not ultimately defined or confined to time or dust, still we must tread the earth and face the birth of dark nights as well as the bright lights of the dawn. Our humanity is umbilical to this beautiful planet and when we examine and experience the earth, air and seas and all that these hold, there begins to unfold the beautiful universes within us. To fully see, smell, hear, taste and touch is to be held in the clutch of our Creator's love and to begin to know of the worlds above.

Spiritual fruits are also the result of knowing and respecting our roots. We come to know who we are by knowing whose we are. To recognize the rock from which we've been hewn, is to prevent us from being strewn to the four winds. To reverence our past is to help us stand fast in the midst of life's storms. From the past comes courage and comfort for the present, hope and direction for the future. We can grow in the flow of history if we carefully discern, choose and chart our course centered in our one true Source — God.

God is Spirit and we are made in His image. We are spirit. Thus, spirituality is our destiny and consequently involves the totality of our life — backward, forward, up, down, in, out. The spiritual path is immersing one's total self in the bath of the refreshing waters of God's love. Spiritual sensitivity and maturity increase when we release our failures (our past), frustrations (our present), fears (our future) to the wisdom and mercy of God and stand faith to faith in His eternal light.

Being

The nature of every reality,
Can never be defined,
The answer to what it means to be,
Can only be divined.

Now

Now listen – intently,
To all the sounds,
That strike the ear,
Then listen to those,
Thou can'st not hear.

Look – discerningly
At all thou dost now see,
Then look,
At what is hidden from thee.

Speak – with gentleness,
To those now near,
Then whisper,
To those who are not here.

Now touch – with love,
The God of love so free,
Then touch,
The one who touches thee.

Perspective

Life with its agenda,
And endless addenda,
Keeps pressing its claims on me,
In the process of choosing,
I find myself losing,
Precious serenity.

But the ebbing and flowing,
The staying and going,
Of life's ever-surging sea,
Makes me serene,
When all is seen,
In the light of eternity.

The Awakening and Expanding of Consciousness

The awakening and expanding of consciousness is one stress of the New Age. There are many ways being tried to attain this goal.

The message of the Christian faith is that Christ is the way to the abundant life through the awakened and expanded consciousness. His thoughts, words and deeds, all in perfect harmony, are the seeds for our integrity.

Through His forgiving love, Christ helps us to move beyond our circle of limitations and condemnations. He breaks open the tomb of restricting resentments and enables us and others to receive resurrection.

Christ's teaching on light — "You are the light of the world" — is a bright ray of hope for those who grope in the darkness of their inferiority and despair. His affirmation of our power is an invitation to scour our fearful faces and with new embraces meet the universe.

To see treasures of heaven, which are measures of leaven in the loaf of eternal life, rather than treasures of earth is to experience a new birth of peace and joy.

Christ's words about not judging is not a "fudging" on decision-making or a "flaking" out of commitment to right. His teaching is mainly a challenge to look within and find the sin which may be hiding in one's own dark shadows.

Christ's healings and His healing word remove much of the absurd from our own consciousness of sickness or health. Often by healing the soul, He teaches the origin of disease is that so often we please to do our will instead of the will of our Maker.

Christ's confrontation with the legalists is a conflict of consciousness — conflict between laws and traditions that bind versus a spirit that is kind; conflict between conformity and controls that diminish versus love that strives to finish all domination by persons, tribes or nations.

Christ's words about lostness lift us from the distress of our aimlessness and hopelessness. The parables of the lost son, lost sheep and lost coin are an invitation to join with Him in the search for self as well as those who are lonely and lost.

The washing of His disciples' feet is Christ's demonstration of the humility of love and His invitation to us to rise above pride and status which so often become the lattice work that imprisons us within and without.

His teachings on the talents (use or lose) provide insights for the gifts of life that are ours. If we bury our gifts in the ground, we are bound to reap weeds or weep in the reeds of the swamps of our consciousness.

Christ says that if we put our hand to the plow we cannot look back from the now. His wisdom is that to live regretfully is to live fretfully with tears in our eyes that dim the glory of our skies of expanded consciousness.

Every extremity illuminates. Christ is God's extremity, awakening, illuminating, expanding our consciousness. He calls us to express glorious thoughts, words and deeds and challenges us to manifest that integrity which comes through the harmony of these three.

Unity at Calvary

Intermingling blood, sweat, tears,
Sight, taste, smell, touch of Calvary,
Lingering taunts and jeers,
The sounds of cruelty.

But beyond the passion and pain of sense,
Another reality,
The experience of non-sense,
The awareness of spirit free.

The meaning of the cross,
Is not shrouded with mystery,
Not counted as gain or loss,
But is ultimate unity.

Is God Odd?

We are so odd,
We nod at God,
And think He will us save.

If only we,
Could see that He,
Does not so behave.

Once on a tree,
For thee and me,
His only Son He gave.

Now sounds His call,
From hall to mall,
Our life for Him to brave.

Still Point

We live in a world of motion, speed and sound — a world of continual cries from commercialism of the market place, of platitudes from pulpits, prescriptions from physicians, warnings from warriors and war-makers, techniques from technologists, subtle secrets from scientists, guarantees, guardianship and guidance from governments. The din is often deafening, the cacophony confusing and we stand before the blaring blasts of the world and its perpetual motion with our hands over our ears and our souls yearning for some stillness, quiet and peace.

But our yearning is not just to be free from motion and sound. This yearning springs deep from the still point within and is the yearning of every soul to find itself in its source, to rest there and to become empowered for new life. For it is this stillness, this centering, this absolutely unmixed attention that provides the creative power, firm purpose and clear direction for each human being.

Silence and centering are essential for entering the process that brings forth the abundant life. The rationale for silence is based on the priority, the firstness of God's word, of God's speaking. God spoke and the universe was created. God spoke and love was born. We are and we love because God acted and loved first. As we listen we learn how to answer.

We are created as hearers of the word of God, conceived in the mind of God as daily partners in dialogue. We bear in our hearts a mystery and that mystery begins to unfold, enrich, enlarge and ennoble through our being still and listening at the center. It is at the stillpoint that we realize the indwellingness of God and know His word is not as truth that is alien to us. God who speaks to us in the silence is not just my best self, but He is the sovereign who elects and disposes according to His will. So we come to the center in faith and risk, not knowing what word will be uttered at that moment.

Centering on God is an act of love which moves beyond thinking and reasoning, for when this kind of contemplation is born, reason dies. Even desires, hopes, fears, ambitions disappear, for ultimately all love is intolerant of reasoned discourse. The heart has reasons that the reason knows not of. It is this love that explains the deep wisdom that accompanies deep silence. Now empty of concepts, the soul is filled with supraconceptual wisdom. The apparent void is filled with a rich wisdom.

It is in the silence that we gird ourselves to meet crises, to make right decisions. If our lives are poured out in many and useless words, we will seldom hear anything in the depths of our hearts. Then when we need to declare who and what we are, we shall be found speechless at the time of crucial decision.

In the silent center we learn to discern and distinguish. Our consciousness is often like a bird that gathers everything that glitters no matter how uncomfortable the nest becomes with all the metal in it. If we are not still, we do not distinguish, do not see clearly and are confused by the glitter and glamour of the world.

Centering enables us to share in the power of God and resonate to the rhythms of life. In the stillness we gain a foretaste of life beyond, a foretaste that lies far beyond the reach of our intellect or so called psychological awareness. It is in this space that we are prepared for the moment of death for as we contemplate our being in silence, we also contemplate our non-being. If death comes to us as an unwelcome stranger, it will be in part because we have not experienced the silence of death in the stillness of our life.

To be still is to become sensitive to the sacrament of all life and the kinship of all. The mystery we discover within our hearts is the mystery within every person's heart. In the very center dwell all our brothers and sisters and the whole creation and there all times — past, present, and future — exist. The person who makes his abode in the center of himself is established at the source of all life. The concern-oriented outward life is ordered and organized from within. Social responsibility and sensitivity is not mere humanitarianism, mere pity, nor mere obedience to Bible mandates. Social concern is grounded in an experience, an experience of the love of God which is so often found in the silence.

So — be still now and know.

Journey Inward

O deep, deep within all,
Where eye can't penetrate,
Is always the mute call,
To come investigate.

To move beyond the seen,
To new worlds without end,
To know another scene,
To with another life blend.

This is the real journey,
Of the truth-seeking soul,
This is the golden key,
That unlocks and makes whole.

Still Point

Amid the flux of strain and stress,
And struggle for earthly power,
I find my strength in mindlessness,
And the still of the twilight hour.

Pause

Life increases its acceleration,
Cacophonous becomes the noise,
It's not speed that brings self-realization,
It's the pause that gives life poise.

Be Still

Life that is filled with flurry and worry,
Is one that's beset with pain,
A life that's constantly moved to hurry,
Is not aware of God's reign.

Be still, be quiet, take time to grow,
In silence and serenity,
Immerse yourself in the gentle flow,
Of God's love and purity.

The Consciousness of a Little Child

Centuries ago a man moved to and fro on planet earth and spoke of a new birth — a spiritual birth that transcends time and space. His message was that the key to this new realm of life was in the consciousness of a little child: "Except that you become as a little child, you cannot enter the Kingdom of Heaven."

What is the consciousness of a little child?

For the child, curiosity is a proclivity. "Why" is a timeless cry. Listen to these pleas from our children. "If you care for me, why do you not fill the aching, hungry spaces in my stomach and why do you not see the vacant, hollow look in my eyes or hear my cries? Why do you often refuse to love me, but choose rather to abuse me and ignore the sobs and throbs of pain that ricochet down the canyons of time into timeless realms of being? Why do you often leave me alone to flaunt your face and lace in the marketplace? Why is your time measured by clocks rather than by rocks of my cradle? Or why do you keep carrying me as a refugee from place to place over waters and desert waste? Why does the sky rain fatal fires of hell instead of gentle waters that bring forth sweet flowers to smell? And if you clone me, will you be any less lonely because I am two? Does more of the same tame the desire to acquire? Does double mean less trouble?"

But all of the questioning curiosity of children is not of morbidity. In the child's simplicity and openness to mystery, there exists an intimacy with the universe that heralds a new kind of destiny for humanity. The child's consciousness of the kinship of all helps us to see a new phenomenon of history. Previously history has progressed through ages and stages in particular partialities. Now the whole world is the problem and challenge. Crucial problems are world problems. A metamorphosis of history has taken place that affects time and space. Here and now is a holistic history of humanity. Ours is a single destiny that points to the necessity for a new spirituality that calls us to transform our hostilities into hospitalities.

Fantasies from the child's mind often bring interruption to our time. These breaks in our routine can be refreshing pauses in our hurried and harried life, causing us to reflect — even genuflect — to the Lord who says, "Be still and know." Much of our desolation and corruption come because we live without much interruption. Amid the wild and furious world of machines and techniques, of speed and greed, of manipulation and consternation, we are whirled about until there is no inner life in us. We become numbers, masks, routines, functions, reputations, successes without a center of gravity. Hollow rather than holy often is our character. The interruptions of the child afford opportunities for us not to take ourselves so seriously — they prick the balloon of our pomposity. There is a divine current that flows through the interrupting mind and heart of a little child that brings a different rhythm to life — a rhythm that leads to stillness and silence where we discover the heart of the Eternal Lover.

The physical love of a child reminds us of the physical love that the peoples of the world so desperately need. There is no way for us to share in the agony of our world, its darkness, shame and confusion except by suffering what it suffers, carrying in our hearts what it carries in its heart. We do not — we cannot become ourselves until we share the deepest level of unity with our death-threatened and oppressed brothers and sisters. We are called by little children to a new consciousness of compassion.

The consciousness of the child contains considerable wonder and awe. The unfolding of a rose, the wiggly worm, the twinkling star carry a child from the confining collectivism of contemporary culture to a communion and community with the cosmos. The micro moments of wonder and awe tell of the majesty and power of the spirit and fill our lives with *kairos* event, i.e., time filled full, which leads to fulfilled lives. Wonder and awe make straw of chronological time and in the timeless moment from our place on the sod we get a glimpse of God and His kingdom. Wonder and awe move us from groveling and groping to cosmic kaleidoscoping.

Play, laughter and joy are so much a part of childhood. In play the child often loses himself or herself in another world, creating a universe of his or her own. Creation is child's play!

Children are trustful. It is this trusting nature that prevents the multiplicity of fears that accumulate with the years. Trust fosters a consciousness that does not entertain limitations that we impose on ourselves or which others suggest for us. Trust moves us beyond the problems of the past and the fears of the future.

Children bear in their bosoms the blessings of hope. The hope of the child is the affirmation that the overwhelming brutality of facts that oppress and repress is not the last word. It is the firm faith that future frontiers are not determined by the limits of the present actual happenings. It is the awareness and caring that we are to plant little oak trees even though we may never gather the acorns. It is to live with a love for those whom we shall never see.

The birth and life of each child is God's clear word that He has not given up on humanity. To love and nurture our children is to be grateful to the Creator of us all.

More Reality

As I observe reality,
Through the senses given to me,
I am aware of a complexity,
A totality,
Of reality,
That is so much more.

So reality comes to me,
Only as partiality,
Shrouded in great mystery,
But with the possibility,
For new creativity,
Beyond this shore.

Healing Memories

As the years come to an end and we begin another, we often remember a friend, spouse, sister or brother who has passed on. To many persons such remembering is mainly mourning for the dead, literally or figuratively placing wreaths at the grave's head, fretting and regretting which bring pain and strain.

But memories can be vehicles of healing, joy and hope if we can direct them rightly. Let your memories of those loved ones who have passed on be a celebrating of life rather than a centering on death, a promoting of love rather than placing lilies, a garnering of gratitude rather than a gathering of grief.

What happens when we remember those who have passed over?

First, we bring the past immediately into our present and make the fact of those past lives a present reality. In memory, we transcend time and space and make historical facts existential moments. We witness to the unbroken chain of life — to the continuity, the on-goingness of the life of the spirit. Just as every Christian acknowledges that Christ is his contemporary, so do we acknowledge that the lives we remember are contemporaneous with our lives.

In addition to professing the continuity of life, our act of remembrance proclaims the kinship of life. The memory of our loved ones reminds us of that fellowship and spiritual kinship that all humans share and enables us to better understand and relate to our fellowmen here and now.

Remembering is also an expression of gratitude — gratitude for life — for those lives we recall and for our own lives. To regard memory as an act of gratitude is to enrich and enlarge the lives of those who are remembered and those who are remembering. For gratitude is giving, and to give is to live. He who lives in an attitude of gratitude knows that latitude of joy and freedom that has no bounds.

Through our memory of others we can often find new courage, hope and strength for ourselves now and in the days to come. Memory can be a catalyst for commitment, a decision for dedication, a renewal of right relationships with God and our fellowmen.

Memory is an act of love — a love that does not fail, falter or forget; a love that creates new life and continues old life; a love that practices the presence of all of life; a love that bridges the canyons of time and space; a love that binds the wounds of severed spirits and frees the minds that are still imprisoned in the caskets of grief.

Thus, memories can be healing if the meaning of memory celebrates life rather than calculates death, utilizes the power of the past for problems of the present and puts in proper perspective the priorities of the present, expresses gratitude for life and gain rather than laments strife and pain, centers life around God rather than focuses on sod, kindles our love rather than spindles threads of bitterness and weaves a web of woe.

To rightly remember is to dismember death and to reaffirm and renew life.

Touching

Salty seas touch the ancient shores,
Barren and bleak,
Each surging wave implores,
The earth to seek,
New dwelling places,
In other spaces,
Far away.

Eternal Spirit touches my soul,
Empty and weak,
Fills, strengthens, makes whole,
And to the peak,
Of ecstasy,
Leads me,
Within.

Nature Mysticism

The mystical experience is an important and interesting aspect of the spiritual life of persons. Some think that the experience is one that begins in mist and ends in schism. However, the genuine mystical experience is just the opposite. It begins in schism and ends in the mist of the mountain top. The schism is one's separation from God, others and self; the mist is that moment of the peak experience where schism gives way to the prism which brings all of the separate colors of spirit into one shining white light. The mystical moment is the prism from which emerges the chrism that crowns the new life — the prism that unites all "isms" into one.

The mystical experience comes by way of many paths. One beautiful path is that of nature, especially as seen in sky, soil and seed.

The sky is more than empty space; it is an expression of God's infinite grace. Cradle of sunset and sunrise, the western and eastern skies remind us of the cosmic and human cycles of death and birth. The moving clouds, driven by the wandering winds, speak to us of the Holy Breath, the Eternal Spirit which carries us over the mountain tops and valleys of life. The heavens at night take us on a flight of fantasy and the countless stars remove the bars of our prisons of egocentricity and complicity with trivia. Playground of fowl, the skies now become a joyful surprise which causes us to sing and wing our thoughts to spaces not yet dreamed of. Lightning and thunder cause us to wonder about the might and majesty of the Deity.

The soil is our mother, from which come son and daughter, sister and brother. The shifting and drifting sands are the earth's hands of time reminding us of our numbered days here. But the regular resurrection from sod tells of our immortal destiny in God. The bounty and beauty that spring from the ground herald the sweet sound of God's voice of love. The treasures from earth's deep bowels are the fulfillment of God's vows to provide for his people. Earth's endless variety is a serendipity that points to infinity. The land on which we walk, crawl, run, leap and stand speaks of the dependability of Deity. Our toil in the soil challenges our ingenuity and offers opportunity for releasing our potentiality and increasing our creativity. Our benevolent relationship to earth brings new birth to body, mind and soul.

The sea is the mirror of eternity. The ceaseless motion of the ocean is like the ever moving watchful eye of God that never closes in slumber or sleep. As the deep throws up and then takes back its foam, we think of our return home to God after our spray of life is finished. Treasures deep down remind us we often must drown to self and its vice before we can find that pearl of great price. The sea's tremendous force points to the power from the Source of all life. The never failing buoyancy communicates the constancy of the ocean of God's love. The sea's countless creatures are primordial preachers of God's wisdom. The sea sweeps us into the mystery of God.

God's beautiful creation is his intriguing invitation to come home to Him — which really is where the mystical path leads.

Divine Gardener

O Divine Gardener –
With tender touch you have tended the earth,
And sowed the seeds of our being,
With warm, sweet breath you have given us birth,
And prepared us for our greening.

But the order you planned, the beauty expected,
Are falling into dread shambles,
For we've greened our own way, your care rejected,
And torn your hand with our brambles.

Snowflake

Delicate dimension of beauty,
Conceived in the mind of deity,
Patterned by the hand of certainty,
Into a matrix of exquisite symmetry,
Dancing delightfully in the span of brevity,
A moment of configuration in eternity,
And then — gone.
Now a tear in the eye of divinity,
A window opening to infinity.

The Quest for Truth

The quest for truth has always been a major motivation and determinant for human behavior. The search is sometimes systematic; often it is erratic and eccentric. Both bane and blessing are fruits of the truth tree quest. The bloody face of history reveals the relentless, and often ruthless, reach for truth. The way is strewn with severed skeletons, battered and broken bodies, muddled and managed minds, scarred souls, and has many turns with twisting trails that torment, torture and tease. But beauty and bounty are also truth's trophies. Placid places, joyful faces and delicate traces of immortality tell of the spell that truth casts upon its pilgrims.

Truth, in whatever form, is many-splendored. No one knows or can reflect all of the splendor. No one knows everything about anything. Like the heavenly galaxies, we see some of the stars, but not all. Like the ever-changing waves of the sea, we glance, catch a glimpse and then they are gone. So it is with the path to truth. We perceive particular partialities. Hardly ever, except maybe in a moment of mystical union, do we know the whole, the pure truth.

Therefore, the search is a process of highest probabilities; that is, the acceptance and application of that reality which is right, reasonable, respectable and responsible for us at a particular time and place in our life's journey. To seek truth in this way fosters freedom, banishes bigotry, allows room for growth of self and others, admits the ranges of changes in life, acknowledges security as frequently fantasy, admonishes us not to be resolute about the absolute and nurtures the human spirit.

In this light, the "horrible" heretics of history become fellow pilgrims and, rather than a cohort that would thwart our journey, or an enemy, offer us another possibility for certainty.

Though truth is beauty, it often appears in dark disguises and comes in subtle surprises. Truth comes to us in work or play, in a lifetime or in a moment, in a cathedral or in a tent, in a bird's song or in a sinner's wrong. Truth may bear its message in pot or in a mess of pottage, in the prose of a rose or in a gory story, in laughter and tears, in faith and in fears, in grief and pain, in sunshine and rain. Truth comes to us through mind and heart, at the end or at the start of life, in war and peace, in retention or release, in prayer and when we care, share or dare. Truth is timeless and timely and is seen in the slave and the free, above and below and in the slow flow of the ages of ice.

We prepare ourselves for the journey toward truth by wearing the garb of gratitude and dress of discipline, carrying the lamp of love, the compass of faith and the staff of hope. We acknowledge the paradoxical possibility and compatability of orderly law and radical randomness, of stability and spontaneity, of the apart-fromness (uniqueness) and the a-part-ofness (commonality) of all creation.

Truth is within and without. We ourselves touch truth when at the end of our journey to the far country we return home to find the treasure we've sought is right there. We come home and there we meet ourselves, we find ourselves already waiting there. To be at home is to be at one with ourselves and with God, the Source of Truth.

The Way

The way to knowledge and wisdom,
To enlightening of the mind,
The way to truth and freedom,
We shall always find,
Is not from classes and books,
Nor from nature's treasure trove,
The way is in the nooks,
Of the heart that is filled with love.

The Leash

Two living beings at the end of a leash,
One with four feet and the other with two,
Now will you tell me if you please,
In this simple scene, who's leading who?

The Teacher

He who stands at the corners of life,
And points to that which is good,
Who enters not into the pain and strife,
Is much like a block of wood.

But he who fearlessly treads the path,
Whose footsteps no power can stay,
Who quietly, patiently stands the gaff,
Is the true teacher who points the way.

Consciousness-Changing

When Spring is near, Mother Earth prepares for birth and we again are mindful of new life. If planet earth is to continue giving birth to and supporting life — especially human life, there need to be new seeds sown in the consciousness of humanity.

Mind and Matter. More and more we seem to be allowing matter to program or rule our minds. Things our minds produce often bring abuse and encourage a recluse life. Machines moving ever faster are becoming our master. Life for many is a menagerie of merchandise sales in which wails and flails are the action — mauls in the malls. Producing and purchasing stuff we're not needing is bleeding our substance and values. Matter and muscle (especially arms) are in constant tussle with the mind and the heart. We need to be more aware of this trend and reaffirm the power and purpose of the mind so that our end will not come with things as our kings. Our challenge is to do less "thinging" and more thinking about what it is to be human on this beautiful planet that is our present home.

Religion and Spirituality. In organized religion there is the tendency to incarcerate the incarnation. The initial revelation often becomes an abomination because the original purity of intent is lost in the wish for security and the bent of a few power hungry persons. Spirit becomes captive to form which is then declared the norm for salvation. Dogma and doctrine become the bastion for bigotry rather than a vehicle that enables one to be free from uncertainty. Those religious institutions that promote prostitutions of priorities by subtle superiorities of theologies and cosmologies are crumbling. Today we need to heed a new way to let the Spirit blow where it will so that each hour the Spirit power can permeate, activate and motivate our entire being.

Mine and Thine. This is the ageless theme and constant dream of persons for power which defoliates the bower of Eden. This symphony of absurdity plays on, "What's thine is mine and I'll take it if I can" and "What's mine is mine and I'll keep it if I can." The dissonance and demonic dance proceed with speed in scores of wars with weapons wiping out our sons — and now our daughters. To replace the sword's blade a new tune must be played, "What's mine is thine and I'll give it if I can." The new consciousness must quickly be the ability to see all humanity as a unity which exists through the creativity of one Father. In this consciousness of the kinship of life, conflict and strife can be transformed to new energy for harmony and liberty.

Our planet is a beautiful place with many a trace of God's grace. We cannot mar earth's face without putting a scar in the space of our mind and heart for we are all part of this creation. Even the far star feels the jar of our deeds, for our actions are fractions of the whole.

So each of us are midwives in the birth that each Spring brings. But we, too, are the ones that are born anew when we allow the plow of God's spirit to break loose the soil of our soul to bear fruit for Him.

Which?

Does the sunset glow outside of me,
Is the rose's fragrance it's own,
Can sourness be in the red cherry,
Does the smoothness belong to the stone?

What of the song of the meadow lark,
Does it really belong to him,
And the energy from the instant spark,
Is it really from within?

Or are the forms of raw beauty,
Which we so often find,
The movement of divinity,
Within the human mind?

Thoughts on Love

Love acts not from facts nor from thinking of love. Love simply is and has within itself its own motiveless source of action. Genuine love does not calculate, cogitate, enumerate or debate. Nor is love based on demand which oft means the hand is closed to those who oppose.

Love is nurtured by truth. Charity is fostered by clarity and honesty is a necessity for love's vitality.

Real love dares to care even when aware that the beloved may reject or strike back. This is the risk of faith in the certainty of the power and victory of God's love. Pure love takes no offense for such love cannot know that which it does not of itself conceive. That which wounds has no place in the kingdom of love.

Love for another is love for oneself. Our own inner transformation is a good demonstration of our love for others. To love and respect one's self is to take from the shelf the sacred bread of self-being and offer it to others as food for their own growth.

The source and goal of love is God. Thus rather than a working out, love is a dwelling in — a dwelling in God. The true self is love. When we live from our authentic identities, we do not hurt or diminish, nor struggle for survival by seeing another as a threat or rival.

No one can fully tell about or explain love for real love is beyond telling. The heart has reasons that the reason does not know and the totality of love is not within the measure or the treasure of the mind. Love, like life, is known as it is experienced by each person, and the experience is the interpreter. The heart beat of love takes place in the bosom of mystery. It is this truth that makes love the greatest power and promise of all eternity.

The Stream of Love

Let your love be free,
As a stream,
That moves between,
The shores of your soul,
And those of your beloved.

A stream that moves,
Over the pebbles of life,
And makes them pearls,
A stream that swirls,
Around rocks of hatred,
And laughs at their powerlessness,
To stop the flow.

A stream that cleanses,
The muddy soil of life's way,
And quenches the thirst,
Of those whose fevered lives,
Make dry their tongues,
And their hearts.

A stream that reflects,
In its clear water,
The brightness of the heavens,
And the smile of God.

The Labor of Love

So strange the ways of love,
So cold the flaming heart,
The nearer to you I move,
The farther we grow apart.

So great is love's joy and gladness,
When to its sweet song I thrill,
But greater yet love's sadness,
When its chalice I cannot fill.

The peaks of love are so high,
That all else fades from my view,
But these heights sometimes deny,
My vision even of you.

Thus true love comes to me,
As gain and yet as loss,
Its message a mystery,
Its way – that of the cross.

Uniqueness

One of the most precious and powerful aspects of creation is uniqueness. God does constantly bless through the uniqueness of his creation which knows no duplication. There are similarities and complementarities, but everything in the universe has its own disparities.

The implications of this fact are most revealing and revolutionary for our lives. To recognize the reality of uniqueness causes us to express a greater appreciation for and understanding of the magnificence and beneficence, the creativity and infinity, the wisdom, humor and love of God. To be aware of the particularity of each person means to realize all come from God "custom made" and that our search to return to God (mankind's religions) may not be laid out in one way. Uniqueness is the creator's dress of beauty. Individuality and singularity are the serendipity of divinity. The unique is not a freak of creation, not the hallucination of divine donation, but the demonstration of God's boundless love and imagination. With every new creation, the cosmic kaleidoscope brings forth an exciting revelation and cause for celebration of our own unique being.

Being sensitive to the uniqueness of others enables us to see our sisters and brothers in a new light. Now each one comes to our eyes as a surprise. There is no place for stereotyping and no longer can we bring judgement because one does not conform to the norm. To recognize the unique helps us develop patience in relationships, especially when the "chips are down." Because of uniqueness, the possibilities for progress and problem solving are endless. The special gifts of each provide opportunities to teach that the holocausts of history need not be repeated. Uniqueness challenges us to be responsive and responsible toward our brothers and sisters — not in whispers — but in voices filled with love.

To be cognizant of uniqueness helps us to deal with our own boredom and stress for we know that circumstances also have their uniqueness as they change in the flow of time. Our uniqueness leads us to profess gratitude for the wonder of self. Gratitude for one's self is the foundation for the affirmation and celebration of life. Uniqueness enables us to experience the gaiety of spontaneity. Individuality tells of the reality of one's place in the totality of creation — in the scheme of God's dream. Thus each life has worth from the moment of birth. Originality is a challenge to ever actualize our potentiality. To know and to be in touch with our uniqueness is to love and bless God, others and self.

Thank God now for the miracle of you!

Conformity

Conformity
Is a tragedy
For humanity;
For you see,
In conformity,
You are not free
To yourself be,
Or to journey
Toward discovery.

Systems

Systems are cisterns
That collect and hold,
The minds of men,
Their blood and gold.

Choices

What is pain? Is it the rain that ruins a planned play day or is it the falling water that penetrates the clogged clay and allows the waiting seed to begin its journey toward its destiny?

What is suffering? Is it the sting of Satan and his ring of victory or is it the hand of divinity giving us new courage to be?

What is failure? Is it the lure that leads us to the end of the trail where we declare that to fail is the finality of our future or is failure another moment of truth which affirms that the proof of life is not perfection, but is the subjection of our will to the One who is perfect.

What is sadness? Is it merely the absence of gladness as darkness covers our soul or is it harmony with humanity in the superb symphony of life?

What is disappointment? Is it the event that comes from our unfulfilled expectations and diminishes our elations and relations with life or is it a lesson that the river of life often flows beyond the banks of our desires and thereby inspires us to new experiences of patience?

What is despair? Is it the bottom of the stair which leads to the dark cellar of our life where the debris of our past is stored or is it the moment of realization that the rejuvenation of life is in the wisdom and power of God?

What is defeat? Is it the retreat to resignation and retiring from our goals and zest for life or is it the knowing that God is showing us that more is to be done before the race that we run will bring the victory we seek?

What is depression? Is it the regression to self-pity, isolation and loneliness or is it, in the dark depths, a rest before we're carried to the crest of the waves in our ocean of life where again we experience the light?

What is fear? Is it the feeling that loss is near or is it the clear signal that new faith is the need so that the seed of trust and hope may grow?

What is guilt? Is it simply the silt from muddy waters of our past or is it a call from within to begin new ways of living and accept God's forgiving love?

What is shame? Is it a way we defame our name or is it a reminder for us to be kinder to ourselves and others in the journey of life?

What is frustration? Is it the encrustration of life's desires or is it the awareness that we have a place in the story of the universe and the verse we write does not always fit the moment we submit it?

No Hiding Place

Too often we try to save face,
When we have failed miserably,
By looking for a hiding place,
In the forests of history.

But forests die and shadows fade,
And soon we stand bare in our sorrow,
I'll choose not to hide in yesterday's shade,
But live in the light of tomorrow.

Christ Consciousness

Christ consciousness is a consciousness of infinite possibilities, a consciousness that is constantly renewing, creating, transforming and restructuring reality at subatomic, biological, psychological, sociological and cosmic levels.

The exquisite excitement, heightened hope and demanding dimensions which such a consciousness offers to us emerge from Christ's words, ". . . he who believes in me will also do the work that I do and greater works than these will he do." Interpreters of these words often by-pass their depth of meaning because they fear that to take these words of Christ seriously demeans and even denies his lordship. Not so. By knowing the potential within all humanity and by expressing his own humility through these words, Christ calls mankind to his highest calling — "to be perfect as your Father in heaven is perfect." When these words of promise and power to do greater things become a Christian's way of life, he too has a consciousness of infinite possibilities.

The consciousness of Christ is a catalyst for ever new syntheses. Christ is an interventionist in the ontological constitution of the universe. Although Christ recognized and respected natural and spiritual laws, he did not regard the universe as a fixed, arrived-at, mechanical unit. He saw the universe as a matrix needing continual resynthesis and renewal. Life was kaleidoscopic and he saw his mission as ever seeking to pattern the pieces for perfect beauty and symmetry. His mind brought cosmic consciousness to bear on ordinary reality so that hollow men might become holy men.

His interventionism was always motivated by human need and directed toward alleviation of suffering. When logic and reason failed to solve human conflicts or chaos, the consciousness of Christ restructured the situation so that resolution of problems and right relationships became possible. His table talk with Zachaeus, his forgiveness of the thief on the cross, his breaking the sabbath, his healing blind Bartimaeus, his changing the water to wine, his raising of Lazarus, his calming the stormy sea, his crucifixion — all bear wonderful witness to the catalytic and interventionistic quality of his consciousness which brought forth new beings.

The Christ consciousness is thus revolutionary and revelationary. Christ did not offer intellectual procedures and explanations for living. This is not to say he broke entirely with logic, law and reason, but rather went beyond, transcended and perfected these approaches to reality. This is the faith which Christ saw as an oasis in the heart which could never be reached by the caravan of thinking. He saw the rational life as dealing with just the surface part of the mind and occluding total awareness. He avoided systems — which are virtually always based on logic — which he knew only became fragments of reality that ultimately fettered, frustrated and fractured man's body, mind and spirit. He knew that it is truth that makes one free and truth can never be realized through reason alone. One of the tragedies of much Christian thought is that it has, consciously or unconsciously, blotted out the consciousness of Christ through dogmas, doctrines and theological systems. Truth for Christ is never a product or system but rather a process, a one-ing with God.

Christ consciousness is the consciousness of community. His emphasis on the potential, value and uniqueness of individuals should not make us lose sight of his deep concern for community. He knew lives were shaped not primarily in isolation, solitude or in relation to things, but in human relationships, especially in covenant community. He knew the meaning of human personality was always related to community and he knew the transcendent quality of human life emerged only as one was in community. He regarded sin as refusal to grant one participation or position in community.

On the other hand, Christ knew that real community has meaning only as individuality prevails. When one's uniqueness and potential are submerged, stifled or suffocated, community becomes demonic and destructive.

The consciousness of Christ is thus not directed primarily to the institution, whatever the form, but to the constitution of the human family, and to the unfolding of human life through the commitment to creative community.

Salvation, in the mind of Christ, is a process of full and rightful self-discovery and self-expression. This can only happen, though, in community with man and God. To love God, neighbor and self is not only the great commandment, but also the way to community and wholeness.

What does Christ consciousness then mean for those who choose to walk along His path? Ultimate commitment. Every aspect of life is to be devoted to the path. Such commitment calls for unambiguous intent. Clarity of mind, honest understanding of one's own motives, singleness of vision are essential.

Ultimate commitment demands the total investment of energies and talents for the way. Such power input, however, has to be freely given, unconditionally and voluntarily surrendered, or else such power can become demonic. This is the danger of egocentric thinking and acting which knocks one off balance and traps one in rigid systems and structures of society. Christ called for a child-like faith, not a childish attitude which is often the manifestation of ego.

Ultimate commitment requires risk, going out on the limb, for this is where the fruit is.

Ultimate commitment requires practicing the presence of God, determined spiritual discipline. *Kairos* event requires *chronos* discipline. *Kairos*, that moment in which God breaks through unexpectedly with life-changing results, becomes possible, understandable and meaningful when *chronos*, day-to-day time set by the clock, has been filled with discipline of the spirit.

Ultimate commitment is ultimate love. Christ knew that at the heart of every human problem is the problem of the human heart.

The Christ consciousness is truly radical, revealing, revolutionary, reverent, responsible and realistic. All of these qualities of life he promises to those who trust him and walk in his path.

Comment on Crucifixion

Not a question of a time and a place,
Is the event of crucifixion,
But an experience of the entire race,
The meaning of the human condition.

For man to be man must always shatter,
The bonds that confine him to earth,
He must die on the cross of matter,
That his real self can come to birth.

Lord Jesus

Come, Lord Jesus, come,
Into our hearts today,
Take, Lord Jesus, take,
The love of sin away.

Turn, Lord Jesus, turn,
Our thoughts to God above,
Help, Lord Jesus, help,
Us to receive his love.

Speed, Lord Jesus, speed,
Our halting steps to thee,
Give, Lord Jesus, give,
To us the victory.

Spiritual Healing

Spiritual healing is questing for wholeness. The key to wholeness in life, to healing, is being in God.

One of the ways we move toward wholeness and healing is through *kenosis*, through emptying ourselves. It is in this emptying process that we move beyond the haze of superficialities, the maze of partialities and the craze of inauthentic crucialities to the still point of the soul. *Kenosis* is a return to the point of beginning. *Kenosis* is the renunciation of the dominion of our own thoughts, words and deeds to the will of God. In that renunciation we then gain all that we renounce on a higher level. We find life by losing life in God.

Kenosis leads to *kinesis* (movement). Kenosis is not an inner journey of renunciation that begins and ends with one's own self. *Kenosis* never exists for its own sake. It is the mother of mighty and miraculous movement. *Kenosis* is the womb that gives birth to freedom — freedom that operates within and beyond space and time and motion categories. *Kenosis* sets up the contact and contract with Eternal Spirit and thereby sets in motion the God force within.

Healing energies do not come to full orchestration and power from the endless sounds and fiddlings of persons. The rhythm, crescendo and symphonic movements of healing energies develop in *kenosis* and then emerge to touch the dying body, mind or spirit with vitalizing vibrations.

Wholeness and healing come about also through an awareness of the ever-newness of God. This means that we are not to continually seek God with preconceived ideas of what or who God is. Recognition of the continual new creationism of God is the catalyst which helps produce hope, joy, gratitude and love — all of which release healing energies. The unending and unanticipatory movement of a lavishly loving God brings renewal to those who stand ready. The majesty and mystery of an ever-creating and ever-renewing God is the motivating power for the attuned head, heart and hand to effect new syntheses and to participate in saving synchronicities. Healing comes about by restructuring the realities, by changing the conditions so that sickness cannot survive. To be awake to the unique moment by moment opportunities that God offers us is to increase our capacity to be channels of healing.

Wholeness and healing are facilitated through one's sensitivity to the unity and sanctity of humanity. Life is God expressing Himself. Human relationships become destructive and human beings become sick when this fact is not understood and/or accepted. To be unaware of the divine origin and direction of life exposes one to the ravages of all the powers of darkness.

We are members one of another. Kinship is our nature. To deny this and to act out this denial is to be unnatural, inauthentic. To be unnatural and inauthentic is to be disintegrated, split, not whole.

Thus healing requires more than one, two, ten or twenty I-Thou relationships. Healing calls for universal I-Thouness, for universal love. Genuine love and reverence (necessities for healing) for one human life can only be possible when love and reverence for all human life exist, for the nature of our being is one.

The Spirit Within

In times of pain and fear,
Of suffering and stress,
We tune our ears to hear,
How others will us bless.

When trials overwhelm,
And we approach despair,
And our life's entire realm,
Seems far beyond repair,
We reach out in expectation,
And hope that we shall find,
Another source of renovation,
Balm for our troubled mind.

But in all our woes and weariness,
Our help has always been,
From the spirit of holiness,
That gently dwells within.

A Touch of Silence

So softly silence surrounds the self,
Severed by sound,
Tenderly touching,
One who has been bound,
By noise of strife and pain,
And words that strive to maintain,
Their power over body and mind.

Then in the gentleness and tenderness,
Of the silent touch,
There comes release,
New joy and peace,
Sought for so much,
And gently, quietly,
One is again free.

Rhythm

All around us God's universe resounds and reverberates with rhythm. Through boundless space we can trace the story of God's glory in the rhythm of sun, star and moon. The whirling, swirling lights bless us with days and nights, with winter, spring, summer and fall, and in the thrill of each season we still our reason as our hearts resonate to the rhythms of the hymns of the universe.

The ebb and flow of the great oceans is a symphony that stirs our emotions. The life that abounds in the depths of the seas plays out its many melodies.

The earth, place of our birth, orchestrates from the ground the ceaseless rhythmic sound of life and death. As we trod the sod, toil in the soil, and hew the stones, we oft are in tune with the tones of our planet.

Within us a universe also abounds with rhythmic sounds. It is the rhythm of the human soul that opens the doors for ever new sacred scores, to new renditions and to welcome transitions to a new harmony for the heart of humanity.

The rhythms of the soul are many. The melody that plays deep within our souls has its rhythmic counterpart in the tolls of the bells for the suffering and dying. We really reach out to others by meeting them in their inner worlds, but this is only possible if we have entered our own inner world. The rhythm of our souls is right when our concern for others issues from the holy center within ourselves.

The rhythms of time and eternity are also soul rhythms. Time, the measurement of the duration of successive moments of life given to us, has meaning and purpose when filled with event and activity which are timeless. When we feed the soul, which is timeless, we make whole the measured moments of life when they are played against the background of timeless truths. To those out of tune and time with the Eternal Director, life is filled with disharmonies, but to those who are in synchronization with the Eternal Source, life is a manifestation of a beautiful melody and a fantastic force.

There is also a soul rhythm of individuality and community. The soul requires the experience and discipline of the solo. The uniqueness of each one of us demands some solitude so that the amplitude of the heavenly harmonies can be heard and assimilated. But life also declares a desire for the choir where the fire that burns within the soul can flame and proclaim the community and unity of humanity. We grow, apart from others, but we know that we flourish together as sisters and brothers. This soul rhythm of aloneness and togetherness produces a symphony of great beauty.

To live is to give. To live is to receive. In the great symphony of life where balance prevails between these two movements, when the rhythms are true and free flowing, then will come the knowing of those harmonies that will soothe our severed souls and synchronize our lives with the melodies from all of God's universe.

Thee – Tree – Me

O God,
As the tree, skeletoned before the sky,
Stands leafless, naked,
Waiting for Thy
Tender touch to cloth her limbs,
And send sweet sap rising
Through her whole being,
So that when gentle rain
And warm sun comes again,
She may be fully treeing.

O God,
So stand I, skeletoned before the sky,
Leafless, naked, bare,
Waiting to become aware
Of your care,
And to know within me
That same energy
Of life and love,
So that when gentle sun and rain,
Or raging storm of pain,
Or when o'er me the cold winds blow,
I may fully know,
My being, my treeing,
In Thee.

Power

One of mankind's greatest challenges has been the use of power. Simply identifying the possibilities, problems, priorities and promises of power is a serious and significant exercise and one that is so necessary in our time to cope with the widened scope of power and to give hope that the bower of humanity will yield good fruit.

The power that cascades from the cosmos is constantly calling and challenging us to cast off our binding traces and explore the unknown spaces beyond and to consider how the far star affects our daily lives. Endless, exciting energies from the skies cause us not only to raise our eyes, but our consciousness as well. We are discovering that power from on high in many ways has a tie-in with life here below. Events on earth are frequently given birth through celestial communications and catastrophes. What is loosed in heaven is loosed on earth.

Power processes and patterns are everywhere seen in the natural history of planet earth. The geological time clock ticks on. Eroding soils reveal the spoils of the power of wind and sea. Continental ice floes, faults, land slides and earthquakes all leave in their wakes multitudes of life forms once energized, but now still as skeleton and fossil.

The power expressed by humankind continues to baffle the mind. The history of humanity is the marvelous story of hand and brain. Through these, humans make tools, weapons, machines and instruments — a myriad variety of extra-corporeal things that can be applied to an endless number of operations in almost any environment. The power production of the mind is evidencing a major emergence in human evolution — a tremendous expansion and transformation of consciousness in perceiving, conceiving, knowing and understanding.

History is holding its breath and the present is detaching itself from the past like a vast iceberg broken from its icy base and turning its face toward uncharted seas. Science and technology are rapidly producing the opportunity for community or chaos. National priorities, provincial particularities, and superficial trivialities are becoming effete and obsolete. The history of humanity has begun and we are now realizing that a single destiny governs the whole. The energy now emerging is a surging of soul power that permeates both macro and microcosm.

We do not always comprehend these many expressions of power but often they apprehend us. How do we respond to the power that each minute, each hour confronts us in the physical, mental and spiritual worlds of being? One important answer is in terms of value and meaning and the postures we can assume are basically two — pessimism or optimism. Is the universe utterly pointless or is there meaning and purpose? Is the future fantastic or foreboding?

For the pessimist, the way is to accept the *status quo*, to say "no" to challenge and change, to settle for comfort, convenience or violence, to drink beer and cheer for victory on T.V. The universe soon devours the pessimist who cowers before the fist of fatalistic finality.

The optimist trusts the "musts" of change which range throughout the universe. This healthy cosmology is the basis of a sound psychology. The universe is not in a conspiracy against mankind, but it is the Creator's benign design for all of us. God leaves his handwriting everywhere and the optimist urges us to learn to read. To rightly use power and to bring to flower our destiny, we are to courageously and persistently strive to break down the barriers that prevent the harriers of harmony from completing the race for unity in whatever space we find ourselves to be. The parenthesis of exclusionism is to be erased and replaced by the exclamation point of acceptance for all.

The optimist calls us to move the energies of our bodies, minds and spirits from a maximization of materialism to a spiritualization of matter. The optimist chooses the way of hope which means to be ready at every moment — even from night to morn — for that which is yet to be born, and all signs of new life to cherish so that the good will not perish.

The optimist knows that the throes and woes of suffering and pain are not in vain, but at the same time ever strives to quiet the cries of those who lament in torment. The optimist is a horsefly that stings the scalp of the intellect and the seat of the soul to prevent them from sleep, which tends to keep power positioned and partitioned in paralyzing and preposterous postures of potentiality rather than actuality.

Power in endless ways and voices persistently presses us to make choices. The ultimate choice of the optimist is that of love — love of God, neighbor and self. The one who chooses these loves does not seek power, nor get into power plays or forays, because such a one already has power.

So in whatever sense we conceive, experience or utilize power, let us realize that the hour is always now to love unconditionally. Then we shall be free and the future will be a marvel of beauty.

The Spirit of Power

Gracious God, who is always near,
Sustaining us every hour,
Has not given the spirit of fear,
But the spirit of total power.

Anger and hatred are not the gifts,
Of eternal spirit above,
But tender touches that heal the rifts,
And gentle expressions of love.

Joy

One of the greatest fruits of the spirit is joy. To manifest joyfulness in one's being is to bring about a freeing from much strain and stress which too often possess our bodies, minds and spirits.

Joy is a blessed balancer which, like a delicate dancer, moves through all levels of our being dissipating disharmonies and bringing new melodies for the symphonies of our daily life. The healing energies of our laughters become the rafters on which we build bulwarks against the stormy seas of sorrows and suffering.

The joyful life is a grateful life. To have joy in one's heart is to start the flow of thanks to the banks of the lives of others — thanks for the happy memories, for present ecstasies and for future possibilities. Joy-filled gratitude is an attitude that is creative. Gratitude creates in others a sense of worth, and thereby gives birth to new joy and meaning.

Joy nurtures hope which is the rope to which we cling when despair tries to fling our lives apart. A heartfelt laugh oft becomes the staff that comforts us as we go through the valley of the shadow of death. Hoping is not groping through the darkness of the future's unknown, but rather hoping is walking ahead on the sod with joy to the throne of God.

The spirit of joy is always around whenever love does abound. The peak experience of lovers is bliss that covers the hurts and hungers. Love for the poor is the door to joy for the lover and the beloved. Happiness is the gentle caress for a fevered brow or the knowing how to love one who has sought to have you undone. Real pleasure is sharing your treasure with those in dire need. Joy lights its torch from the flame of love and the fire of love is fanned by the gentle breeze of joy.

Love leads us to truth, so joy shares in the journey that makes us free. When truth is known, inexpressible joy is shown in body, mind and spirit.

Joy as a fruit of the spirit has no time or space limit. Joys that come from the life beyond become the frond which fans away the foreboding fears of death. The joys of heaven are the leaven for raising our loaf of life here and now. Memories of joys from the far past enable us to cast new molds for our life. Joy can be the key to free the lonely from their prisons.

Thus joy is a formidable force and its ultimate source is God. God is the joyful and playful Creator in every theater of life. He is the happy Father who tickles his children with tender touches and often clutches them to His breast where they rest each moment in the deepest content. God is the blissful Lover who warms and blesses all with the cover of His mantle of love.

The joyous life is life in God. The treasure of pleasure is soon lost and the cost is great when God is not known. Happiness is a flimsy dress which is soon rent when God is not present in one's life. Joy is a worthless alloy, a broken toy, a plaintive ploy when the Lord of life is a gimmick in our employ. Contentment is soon spent when the One who has lent us life for awhile is only a pile of stones before which we kneel. Without God as the center of lives, gladness soon becomes sadness and our grief becomes the reef on which our ship of life is wrecked.

In your life joy will abound when you let yourself be found by the Hound of heaven whose constant chase is to find you and erase your fears and lead you, or pull, so that your joy may be full now and forever.

Rejoice and be glad in the Lord.

The Face of Joy

O joy I ever seek your face,
To make my heart rejoice,
In the rare and commonplace,
I strive to hear your voice.

But your face and voice elusive are,
And oft my quest seems in vain,
But then the truth from afar,
That in God's love I remain.

My heart is glad and joy comes full force,
When this awareness comes to me,
That oneness with God is joy's only source,
For now and eternity.

Joy of Life

O Eternal Spirit –
Earth, sky, sea,
Every part of Your creation,
Pulsates with Your energy,
Vibrates with great elation.

O Eternal Spirit –
I, too, pulsate to Your power,
And rejoice that you've given me,
Each week, each day, each hour,
Life that flows so free.

Thoughts on Creation

Silence is the womb of creation. All forms and expressions of creation are conceived in the silence of the consciousness of the Creator. Growth before birth is usually quiet. Brooding and nesting, pondering and wondering are silent sentinels protecting the unfolding forms of life. The rising sun brings forth a new day in heavenly silence. The seed silently pushes through the sod revealing the power of God and the pregnant billowy clouds release their silent snow-flake offspring without uttering a sound. The birth of love always comes through the unspoken word of the heart.

So live often in the deep silences of your being and you shall experience new creations within the universe of your heart, mind and soul and begin to know something of the goal which the creator sets before you.

Creation is purposeful power. Creation is intentional. Patterned in the wisdom of God, every particle portrays directed energy and though the dance may often seem like chance, purpose persistently prevails. Every part of you and the whole of you are made to be played in the divine symphony. To know this, to live this truth is not only to discover the heart of the Lover, but also to be in harmony with humanity and to be aware of your own destiny. It is sensitivity to this aspect of God's creativity that makes you free.

Creation knows no duplication. Each is unique and no matter how diligently you seek, you shall never find two of a kind. The mystery of the history of all forms of creation is the source of the force that produces gratitude for your unique being. Your special individuality is the key to personal responsibility and ultimately to peace, hope and joy. Your uniqueness is the caress of the Maker's hand and challenges you to stand firm in the identity that is yours alone.

Creation is an act of divine love. As such there is never a cessation of creation. In the heavens and on the earth, birth always prevails because God's love never fails. When you love as God above, you join him in his creation. This is the most precious privilege and highest honor that your Creator gives you — to be a co-creator in the boundless theater of his universe. You are ever called to be an actor on the stage on which the drama that is played out has no age and in which the only curtain is your uncertain will to fulfill your role.

Therefore, seek to find through your heart and mind the meaning of your creation, the reasons for your being so that right here and now you can be freeing yourself and others from the chains and pains of aimlessness and distress and move forward with resolve to help solve the pressing problems that perplex and preclude us all from the kingdom of God.

Stones

Stones
Are the bones
Of Mother Earth;
If you would have new birth,
Cast not stones at another,
Your brother,
But gather stones together with true intent,
To build of them a monument,
To the heart of the Lover,
And there discover,
Your own.

Creation

The limitless void,
In all of its darkness and silence,
Awaits to be filled
With light and sounds
Of love.

Divine love,
Stirring and yearning
To create new heavens and earths,
Now struggles for births
Beyond number.

The void,
Now yields to the motion,
The still emptiness,
Now an ocean
Of total love,
Merging and surging,
Bringing forth together,
In a scintillating dance of joy,
The waters of our life;
And the Spirit of God
Moves over the face of our waters.

Dreams — Windows to the Soul

Some of the mystery of the history of humanity in general and of our own personal history in particular can be understood through dreams. For dreams are like beams of lights that penetrate the dark nights of our puzzlements and plights. The trouble and rubble which within us are teeming are often released through our dramatic dreaming. But pleasure and beauty, rich treasure and duty are also the harvest and the gleaning of dreaming. In the dark waters of sleep, dreams take us to the quarters of the deep where we find precious pearls of the mind and also discover the hidden heart of the Lover. It is in dreams, too, that we are brought to a new realization of the common origin and destination of all creation. This leads to an emancipation from the futile frustration of self-adulation.

Dreams can be revelations from God that provide elevations from sod and which enable us to table at His banquet. These divine intimations are sublime invitations to new birth here on earth. In dreams, God effaces the troubling traces of times and places and bears us to boundless spaces, revealing fantastic or favorite faces where time is not. In dreams, God parts the seams of His veil and we see scenes of heaven which provide the leaven for the bread of life here and now. Dreams are the nod of God for us to trod in His path, to play and to laugh with the stars.

In dreams, we discover our sister and brother are not just of our species or race. Though our physical birth is of earth, our soul is a part of the whole. In dreams, visions of strange creatures become the preachers of the commonality of creativity. Silent, scintillating symbols point beyond fantasy to the holistic history of our humanity and present a kaleidoscope of hope. For to know we are one is to have begun that journey for which our hearts burn and our souls yearn.

Dreams help us to understand that vast land of our own pilgrimage. In our waking state, there accumulates a spate of fears and frights, tears and flights, joys and plays, ploys and forays; our challenges with sex and the whole complex of relationships. Dreams help to caress the pain of stress, to help us know some of the "why" of the flow of events, to help us uncover the forces that smother the breath of life each day and keep us at bay from the fountain of truth. Dreams are the bubbles that raise the garbage and rubbles from the stagnant swamps of our deep and thereby help us to keep the stream of living water flowing throughout mind and soul. Dreams are cleansing streams for the subterranean caverns which harbor the concerns of our day to day living.

Our bodies, wracked with pain and frustration, use dreams for release. Distorted energies within our bodies can be made straight through the gate of dreaming. Dreams can bring healing through the revealing of hidden maladies and broken melodies within the symphonies of our bodies. In dreams, our minds are made calm, and there oft comes a balm for our wounds.

Dreams are windows to the soul which open to the whole of life. As we awake each day to its beauty, its glory, we begin to write another story in our book of life. As we retire at night, we gain new sight to read and to heed the stories we write.

Dreams

Night after night it seems,
My soul is filled with dreams,
Yet when the dawns break,
And I awake,
No remnants remain.

Day after day it seems,
My soul is filled with dreams,
But they too,
Do not come true,
For I am unaware.

Lord, in waking or sleeping,
In thy keeping,
May I ever be,
Then my dreams,
Shall be the streams,
Of thine e'erflowing sea.

Walks

On the Mountaintop and Into the Valley

Creation

Consider the fact that there was a point in time when you did not exist on this plane(t) as you now do; that God, through his love and will, caused you to be and has enabled you to be to this moment.

Ponder and praise — think and thank.

Consider that there was a time not very long ago that you did not exist on the plane of consciousness that you are now on; that God, through his love and will, enabled you to be re-created by the movement of his Spirit in your body, mind and soul.

Now see yourself as a new creation with new responsiveness to life and new responsibilities for your life. Depths of darkness and confusions of chaos are giving way to the creating word of God as he speaks to and through you and brings forth light, love and life with new order.

Open your heart, mind and soul to the continuing creation going on within you and let your new heavens and your new earths renew all of creation around you.

Resolve in every thought, word and deed to heal, not hurt; to increase, not diminish; to love, not hate; to bring light, not darkness; joy, not sorrow; peace, not strife; hope, not despair. Be a co-creator with God.

The Center of Life

O Lord, how beautiful is thy creation,
A manifestation of thy great love,
But more beautiful is thy revelation,
Of yourself in our above.

O Lord, who art the source of our very life,
In thee our beings are true,
Your gifts around us too often bring strife,
Unless we center in you.

Communion — Communication

To receive light from another and not to share that light with others is, in effect, to extinguish it. To receive love from God and to not love others is, in effect, to let love die in the tomb of self.

You are given gifts so that they may bear fruits of the spirit. Your talents are treasures of life that are lent to be spent, for the glory of God and for the well-being of his children. The opportunities you are given are doors to pass through and bring others with you.

You are now experiencing new light and love, gifts and talents, opportunities, and bringing forth new concepts and percepts for your on-going pilgrimage; and others are right now emerging, maybe even surging, to be expressed and to be communicated to other life forms.

Feel now those energies that strive to be alive for others. Discern those forces in you that yearn for a new face, a new place to bless. Then with care, dare to share. Let others get a glimpse of the vivifying view from the mountain top. Give of your new being to them. You will thereby be communicating to them the fundamental sacrament of life which is sharing the heavenly bread of self-being. Your joy will be full.

Life is Now

The breath of life God gives to me,
Is subject to his will,
He calls me to speak tenderly,
Before my lips be still.

The thread of life is slender,
My time of life is brief,
So I am now to render,
Where'er I can, relief.

Now is the time to share,
My gift of life so blest,
Now is the time to bare,
My love to those oppressed.

Commitment

To commit is to submit to the Lord of life. Commitment is to allow yourself to be sent.

You are now experiencing new learnings for your mind, yearnings of your soul and bright burnings of your heart. From these dynamics come some strange lands to explore and new hands to clasp in common commitment. The expansion of your consciousness calls you to deeper descents into the wells of your being where the water of life waits to quench your thirst for truth. The mysteries of mind and matter challenge you to launch out into uncharted waters. Both the insearch and outreach call for new commitments to faith — faith that dispels the fog of fear and frustration.

Commitment is the necessary step to one-ing with God and homing in on self. It is the door to intentional living which opens to you worlds of wonder.

Resolve now and in the days ahead to recommit yourself to those previous precious promises still unfulfilled. Commit yourself to new true paths that have been revealed to you. Let yourself be sent and in the descent or ascent trust the truth that in your commitment to the Lord your plans will be established.

Living for God

One lesson of life you should know,
Is to do all things for God,
And not care about the blow,
Of those who think you odd.

For God is our greatest lover,
Source of life that never ends,
In living for Him we discover,
The joy for which all life tends.

Change

Change is the way of all life. Impermanence and insecurity are inescapable and inseparable from life. To accept this truth and to act it out in your life enables you to go with the flow of life and to find harbors of happiness and havens of hope in your voyage through the seas of life. To remain in the *status quo* is to say, "No" to life.

The changes you are undergoing are many. Some carry you through swift currents of confusion or rapids of radical and revolutionary revelations. Other changes bear you to new ports of promise and some cast you adrift on the desert island of doubt, disappointment or discouragement. Some changes bring new calm to the raging seas of your life and sunrises of surprises to the dark night of your soul.

Consider then that change is a blessing for it constantly directs you back to the changeless Source — the Source that enables you to live abundantly. Consider also how the changes in concepts, consciousness, compassion and communication which you experience are the notes that can form the symphony of yourself for tomorrow and how the seeds sown, whether they germinate soon or late, can beautify the garden of your life.

Resolve to assimilate and integrate those changes which enrich, please and give purpose. And those which do not, set them aside but do not destroy them, for in the tide of time they may yet bring to the shores of your life precious cargoes of joy, peace and power for yourself and others.

River of Life

Do you flow with the river of life,
That moves steadily toward the great sea,
Even though it's oft cluttered with strife,
And made ugly with human debris?

Or do you in still pools find your place,
Where everything seems so at rest,
And there appears no ripple nor trace,
Of sorrow, of strife, strain or stress?

The river runs free toward the great sea,
The pool is locked in the land,
The river flows to eternity,
The pool dries up in the sand.

Comfort

To comfort is to give strength. Climbing the mountain is strenuous but strengthening. The process purifies, the vision from the top verifies the value of the climb. The new perspectives from the altitude provide new priorities, possibilities and purposes for your life now. The comfort from the *then* experience can be yours *now*.

The extent of the strength for you is limitless. As you remember, you activate the flow of energy you received from the vast views. As you feel in your consciousness the tender touch of heart or hand of persons who shared your journey and who helped you up steep slopes, you experience strength of body and mind. As you listen to the words which were spoken, you hear more acutely the voices of those calling for your comforts to strengthen them.

Valleys are sometimes dark and desolate, depicting death and despair. When you walk in the valley of the shadows — your own or others' — remember the light from the mountain. When weakness and waste weave their spell over the lives of persons living in the lowlands, you can bring strength, purpose and preservation to them from the highroads you've walked.

Courage is to have heart. Resolve to be courageous so that you can offer comfort to the weak and weary, to the hopeless and helpless and to all in need.

To comfort (strengthen) another is to comfort (strengthen) self.

New Humanity

When one opens his life,
To the pain, stress and strife,
Of others –

When one can,
Call all men,
His brothers –

Then we shall see,
Humanity,
Reborn.

Cherish

Cherish the days and the ways you spend your life. They are precious happenings that will permeate your life with meaningful memories. Cherish them by living in an attitude of gratitude, by letting the glow continue to warm your heart and the light to guide you.

Cherish the persons who now dwell in the city of your consciousness. Let their beings remind you of the unity of humanity and the joy of friendship. Cherish the learnings from them and allow them to join hands and walk with your learnings of the past and of the future. Cherish the choices you made even though not all were the best. To be able to make a choice is a blessing. Cherish the opportunity given to you to be present with others and cherish those who make such opportunities possible.

Resolve to live thankfully now no matter what the vicissitudes of the valley. Practice praise, lavish love, serve God. Then as new happenings come for you to cherish, you will not perish from indifference or indecision.

Epistle to Everyone

The deeper I go,
Into the flow,
Of divine energy,
The more I find,
This life of mine,
Is a part of thee.

The more I discover,
The heart of the Lover,
Of all eternity,
The more I have found,
That I am bound,
To the love of thee.

Continuation

Life is lived in levels, in progressions, in stages, in steps. Cause and effect reflect the flow of life. Companion to change is continuity. Your experience now is the continuation of your experience before. To recognize the relationship is essential for order, progress and direction. You often move forward by looking backward. What is past is prologue.

Continuity is important for you right now because of the significance of your recent past. Perhaps, it was there and then that you opened yourself to new ideas and persons, risking ridicule or rejection as well as hoping for renewal and reinforcement. In these dynamics of faith, you discovered new confidences that provide direction for and devotion to new causes. In your being vulnerable, you allowed a vacuum for vultures to enter in to devour. But that choice now provides a voice in the wilderness of your soul that dispels fear of failure or falling away. The kaleidoscopic content of your mountaintop experiences offers new patterns and paths for your walk in the valley.

The continuity between past and present calls for discipline to develop and grow — the discipline of discernment, of prayer and praise, of study and service, the discipline of remembering and integrating new learnings with old knowledge.

The mountain top experience in your past is not a once-and-for-all one; it is an on-going one that will nurture you now if you will let it.

To Remember

To remember is not to dismember,
The past from the present day,
To remember is to engender,
New life from old clay.

To remember is to place the cut flower,
In waters of life-giving stream,
To remember is to create a new bower,
Where the real presence replaces the dream.

To remember is to take from the shelf,
The bread that has not been broken,
To remember is to hear for oneself,
The word that once was spoken.

To remember is not a regression,
A communion with that which is dead,
To remember is real resurrection,
And power for new life ahead.

Kinship

Behind all existence there is God,
So I am brother to the sod,
And also am I ever kin,
To the never-ceasing wind.

The pulse of life in the surging sea,
Is the same power that moves me,
The mountains stretching toward the sky,
Partake of my own destiny.

The fragrant flower that blossoms forth,
Grows with me from the same earth,
The marvelous lights in the heavens above,
Are partners with me in the dance of love.

Whatever I do, wherever I be,
I am, with all else, of divinity.

Epilogue

You have now walked on the mountain and through the valley. You have not walked by yourself. God and his universe have been your companions. It is in this kinship of all creation that you have known that you are never alone. Rejoice and take heart and, whether on the mountain or in the mart, feel the flow of God's universe in your heart, mind and soul. This is wholeness!

Amblings

In the Garden of Peace

Peace . . .
With Loved Ones

Visualization:

Relax and visualize the faces and figures of family members and friends. Embrace them and offer to them a blessing of love and peace.

Affirmation:

Repeat three times quietly, "God's gifts of family and friends bring to me joys, hopes and peace. Thank you, God."

Prayer:

Dear God, for the precious and sacred lives and loves of those who have moved in the circle of my life, I thank you. For comforting and inspiring memories, for present experiences and for hopes of good relationships in the days to come, I praise your name. Enable me to ennoble the lives of loved ones by kind thoughts, gentle words and peaceful deeds. Help me to forgive and to give for their well-being, to understand and to stand under them when they need support, to rejoice with those who rejoice and to weep with those who weep so that in all of our experiences together we may keep in our consciousness the charge from you that we are to bless one another. I offer myself as an instrument of your peace now for the wholeness of family and friends.

Amen

Peace . . . With the Universe

Visualization:

Relax and image the midnight sky spangled with myriads of stars. Feel the immensity of distance. Then picture a tiny bee sucking nectar from a flower and listen to its gentle buzzing. Feel the steady pulse beat in your wrist. Be aware of your breathing. Finally, realize that the energy, light and life pulsating from the stars, the bee and within you are all one.

Affirmation:

Repeat softly three times, "All of God's creations are my relations and I join with them in praising God for his order, constancy and faithfulness."

Prayer:

O God, Maker and Master of the measureless universe, I praise you for your goodness and greatness, for your majesty and mystery, and for the multitude and magnitude of your mighty acts. I thank you that you have made me to be a meaningful part of your creation and that in this realization of purpose, you have given me peace of mind and soul. Help me to be gentle and kind, aware of and sensitive to all that you have created so that each creature will speak to me of your being. In this kinship of all, I hear and heed your call to be a channel for peace and harmony in your universe.

Amen

Peace . . . With Others

Visualization:

Relax and picture a pink, soft, warm, smooth, sweet-smelling little baby in your arms. Bend your head and gently kiss the tender cheek and feel your love for the infant.

Affirmation:

Repeat to yourself quietly three times. "God is the Father-Mother of all persons. Therefore, all persons are my brothers and sisters and I love them."

Prayer:

Dear God, I thank you for the countless ways you have revealed your love for me and shown me how to love others. I especially thank you for Jesus Christ, the Prince of Peace, the one who has broken down the walls of hostility among persons. In his spirit help me to sound the note of harmony in the symphony of humanity, to never cease to speak and act for peace and to continue to pray for that day when men will lay down their arms and join hands in the circle of brotherhood. O God, help me now to turn any swords I have into plowshares that I may cultivate the hardened soils of humanity so that the fruits of love, joy, peace, patience, kindness, goodness, gentleness, faith, and self-control may flourish on planet earth.

Amen

Peace . . . With Myself

Visualization:

Relax and picture a still lake, snowcapped mountains in the distance and the sun rising and painting the sky with a rosy hue.

Affirmation:

Repeat three times quietly to yourself, "The perfect peace of God is in me, through me, with me, around me and for me, and where God's peace is, no turmoil or conflict can exist."

Prayer:

O God, Still Point of all that is, Source of the peace that passes all understanding, I thank you for your balm for my stressed body, your calm for my stirred-up mind, and your psalm for my anxious soul. I thank you for your promise never to forget nor forsake me and in that promise I now gain the strength and will to still storms that seek to rise within. I yield my restlessness, my fretting, and regretting to your tender touch and clutch your hand so that my walk and talk can be those of peace and love.

Amen

Peace . . . With God

Visualization:

Relax and feel yourself stretched out under the sun on a soft blanket on a warm beach, listening to the lapping waves and watching white sea gulls gliding against a background of blue sky.

Affirmation:

Say to yourself three times, "I am one with God and all creation, at peace, in harmony and free from all care."

Prayer:

Dear God, Central Peace and Calm of the universe, I thank you for your being and for your making me in your image so that I can commune and communicate with you. I thank you for your constant caring, comforting and consoling presence which enables me to be at peace with you. Help me to continually center in you so that I may have the courage and the strength to be an instrument of your peace now and always.

Amen

Home Again

Home Again

O God, Eternal Spirit, receive now my offerings of praise and love and thanksgiving for Your power that creates and controls all of life; for Your peace that brings buoyancy and balance to sinking and unsettled souls; for Your presence that is permanently postured; and for Your promises that always are firm and faithful.

Dear Lord, You who are unanticipatory Ever-Newness, with eager expectation and high hopes, I look to the newness that is to be mine as I seek to better understand the majesty, mystery, and the miracle of mankind. Help me to gain glimpses of immortality as I gaze beyond the glaze of partiality and strike off the tentacles of temporality.

O God, Author of all, in this new chapter of my life, please punctuate perfectly my purposes. With Your word of truth, stir me to question-mark my motives, to put periods behind my perversions, to exclamation-point my priorities, to italicize my faithfulness, to bracket my selfishness, and to erase my pride — so that others who read me may know something of You.

O Lord, in the midst of my joys and successes, make me mindful of the sorrows and failures which engulf me because of the escalation of evil. May I not just be a bystander to the horrors that harrass me. Open my lips and move my body that I may speak and act for justice and mercy. Help me to dispel the false rhetoric of hollow men by my words of truth. Enable me to keep priorities in proper perspective and may the pressures of the present not erase from my mind the values of the past or the hopes of the future. Heal me of my color-blindness so that I may clearly bring to the world the vision that freedom is the birthright of persons of all races. Cure my deafness that I may hear the cries of the suffering and comfort them. Make me, O God, an incisive instrument of Your peace.

Here and now, O God, I commit myself anew to You. I come to this moment in an attitude of gratitude so that I may know and experience that latitude of joy and freedom that only You can give. Dear Lord, in Your love I now abide and I am home.

A Few More Steps

My own journey on planet earth has had many beautiful pathways. Walks and work in office, factory, farm, hospital, campus and church have enabled me to know and love many precious people, exposed me to perilous and productive passages and helped me to realize and love God as the source, force and course of my life.

My paths in government, the military and politics have taught me about the prostitutions of power, the pressing priorities for peace and the beauty of compassionate concern and commitment.

The paths I have walked with my wife and three children have brought bountiful blessings.

Now as I walk on, my journey becomes even more blessed. For you, who have shared some of your life with me through this book, have joined me in the journey toward God.

Louis Richard Batzler

Frederick, Maryland
May, 1982